JAPANESE GIRLS AND WOMEN

BY

ALICE MABEL BACON

GORDON PRESS

NEW YORK
1975

GORDON PRESS—Publishers
P.O. Box 459
Bowling Green Station
New York, N.Y. 10004

Library of Congress Cataloging in Publication Data

Bacon, Alice Mabel, 1858-1918.
  Japanese girls and women.

  Reprint of the ed. published by Houghton Mifflin, Boston.
   1. Women--Japan. 2. Japan--Social life and customs--1868-1912. I. Title.
HQ1762.B33   1975   301.41'2'0952   75-31925
ISBN 0-87968-253-1

Printed in the United States of America

To

STEMATZ, THE COUNTESS OYAMA,

IN THE NAME OF OUR GIRLHOOD'S FRIENDSHIP, UNCHANGED AND

UNSHAKEN BY THE CHANGES AND SEPARATIONS OF OUR

MATURER YEARS,

This Volume

IS AFFECTIONATELY DEDICATED.

PREFACE.

It seems necessary for a new author to give some excuse for her boldness in offering to the public another volume upon a subject already so well written up as Japan. In a field occupied by Griffis, Morse, Greey, Lowell, and Rein, what unexplored corner can a woman hope to enter? This is the question that will be asked, and that accordingly the author must answer.

While Japan as a whole has been closely studied, and while much and varied information has been gathered about the country and its people, one half of the population has been left entirely unnoticed, passed over with brief mention, or altogether misunderstood. It is of this neglected half that I have written, in the hope that the whole fabric of Japanese social life will be better comprehended when the women of the country, and so the homes that they make, are better known and understood.

The reason why Japanese home-life is so little understood by foreigners, even by those who have lived long in Japan, is that the Japanese, under an appearance of frankness and candor, hides an impenetrable reserve in regard to all those personal concerns which he believes are not in the remotest degree the concerns of his foreign guest. Only life in the home itself can show what a Japanese home may be; and only by intimate association — such as no foreign man can ever hope to gain — with the Japanese ladies themselves can much be learned of the thoughts and daily lives of the best Japanese women.

I have been peculiarly fortunate in having enjoyed the privilege of long and intimate friendship with a number of Japanese ladies, who have spoken with me as freely, and shown the details of their lives to me as openly, as if bound by closest ties of kindred. Through them, and only through them, I have been enabled to study life from the point of view of the refined and intelligent Japanese women, and have found the study so interesting and instructive that I have felt impelled to offer to others some part of what I have received through the aid of these friends. I have, moreover, been encouraged in my work by reading, when it was already more than half completed, the following words from Griffis's "Mikado's Empire:"—

"The whole question of the position of Japanese women — in history, social life, education, employments, authorship, art, marriage, concubinage, prostitution, benevolent labor, the ideals of literature, popular superstitions, etc.— discloses such a wide and fascinating field of inquiry that I wonder no one has as yet entered it."

In closing, I should say that this work is by no means entirely my own. It is, in the first place, largely the result of the interchange of thought through many and long conversations with Japanese ladies upon the topics herein treated. It has also been carefully revised and criticised; and many valuable additions have been made to it by Miss Umé Tsuda, teacher of English in the Peeresses' School in Tōkyō, and an old and intimate friend. Miss Tsuda is at present in this country, on a two years' leave, for purposes of further study. She has, amid her many duties as a student at Bryn Mawr College, given much time and thought to this work; and a large part of whatever value it may possess is due to her.

I would say, too, that in the verification of dates, names, and historical incidents, I have relied altogether upon Griffis's "Mikado's Empire" and Rein's "Japan," knowing that those two authors represent the best that has been done by foreigners in the field of Japanese history.

This work also owes much, not only to the suggestions and historical aids contained in the "Mikado's Empire," but to Mr. Griffis himself, for his careful reading of my manuscript, and for his criticisms and suggestions. No greater encouragement can be given to an inexperienced author than the helpful criticism of one who has already distinguished himself in the same field of labor; and for just such friendly aid my warmest thanks are due to Mr. Griffis.

A. M. B.

HAMPTON, VA., *February*, 1891.

CONTENTS.

CHAPTER	PAGE
I. Childhood	1
II. Education	37
III. Marriage and Divorce	57
IV. Wife and Mother	84
V. Old Age	119
VI. Court Life	138
VII. Life in Castle and Yashiki	169
VIII. Samurai Women	196
IX. Peasant Women	228
X. Life in the Cities	262
XI. Domestic Service	299
Epilogue	327

JAPANESE GIRLS AND WOMEN.

CHAPTER I.

CHILDHOOD.

To the Japanese baby the beginning of life is not very different from its beginning to babies in the Western world. Its birth, whether it be girl or boy, is the cause of much rejoicing. As boys alone can carry on the family name and inherit titles and estates, they are considered of more importance, but many a mother's heart is made glad by the addition of a daughter to the family circle.

As soon as the event takes place, a special messenger is dispatched to notify relatives and intimate friends, while formal letters of announcement are sent to those less closely related. All persons thus notified must make an early visit to the newcomer, in order to welcome it into the world, and must either take with them or send before them some present. Toys, pieces of cotton, silk, or crêpe for the baby's dress are regarded as suitable; and these must be accompanied by dried fish or eggs, for good luck. Where eggs are sent, they are neatly arranged in a covered box, which may contain thirty, forty, or even one hundred eggs.[1] The baby, especially if it be the first one in a family, receives many presents in the first few weeks of its life, and at a certain time proper acknowledgment must be made and return presents sent. This is usually done when the baby is thirty days old.

Both baby and mother have a hard time of it for the first few weeks of its life. The baby is passed from hand to hand, fussed over, and talked to so much by the visitors that come in, that it must think this world a trying place. The mother, too, is denied the rest and quiet she needs, and wears

[1] All presents in Japan must be wrapped in white paper, although, except for funerals, this paper must have some writing on it, and must be tied with a peculiar red and white paper string, in which is inserted the *noshi*, or bit of dried fish daintily folded in a piece of colored paper, which is an indispensable accompaniment of every present.

herself out in the excitement of seeing her friends, and the physical exercise of going through, so far as possible, the ceremonious bows and salutations that etiquette prescribes.

On the seventh day the baby receives its name.[1] There is no especial ceremony connected with this, except that the child's birth is formally registered, together with its name, at the district office of registration, and the household keep holiday in honor of the event. A certain kind of rice, cooked with red beans, a festival dish denoting good fortune, is usually partaken of by the family on this occasion.

The next important event in the baby's life is the *miya maéri*, a ceremony which

---

[1] A child is rarely given the name of a living member of the family, or of any friend. The father's name, slightly modified, is frequently given to a son, and those of ancestors long ago dead are sometimes used. One reason for this is probably the inconvenience of similar names in the same family, and middle names, as a way of avoiding this difficulty, are unknown. The father usually names the child, but some friend or patron of the family may be asked to do it. Names of beautiful objects in nature, such as Plum, Snow, Sunshine, Lotos, Gold, are commonly used for girls, while boys of the lower classes often rejoice in such appellations as Stone, Bear, Tiger, etc. To call a child after a person would not be considered any especial compliment.

corresponds roughly with our christening. On the thirtieth day after birth, the baby is taken for its first visit to the temple. For this visit great preparations are made, and the baby is dressed in finest silk or crêpe, gayly figured, — garments made especially for the occasion. Upon the dress appears in various places the crest of the family, as on all ceremonial dresses, whether for young or old, for every Japanese family has its crest. Thus arrayed, and accompanied by members of the family, the young baby is carried to one of the Shinto temples, and there placed under the protection of the patron deity of the temple. This god, chosen from a great number of Shinto deities, is supposed to become the special guardian of the child through life. Offerings are made to the god and to the priest, and a blessing is obtained; and the baby is thus formally placed under the care of a special deity. This ceremony over, there is usually an entertainment of some kind at the home of the parents, especially if the family be one of high rank. Friends are invited, and if there are any who have not as yet sent in presents, they may give them at this time.

It is usually on this day that the family send to their friends some acknowledgment of the presents received. This sometimes consists of the red bean rice, such as is prepared for the seventh day celebration, and sometimes of cakes of *mochi*, or rice paste. A letter of thanks usually accompanies the return present. If rice is sent, it is put in a handsome lacquered box, the box placed on a lacquered tray, and the whole covered with a square of crêpe or silk, richly decorated. The box, the tray, and the cover are of course returned, and, curious to say, the box must be returned unwashed, as it would be very unlucky to send it back clean. A piece of Japanese paper must be slipped into the box after its contents have been removed, and box and tray must be given back, just as they are, to the messenger. Sometimes a box of eggs, or a peculiar kind of dried fish, called *katsuobushi*, is sent with this present, when it is desired to make an especially handsome return. When as many as fifty or one hundred return presents of this kind are to be sent, it is no slight tax on the mistress of the house to see that no one is forgotten, and that all is properly done. As special messengers are sent, a number of men are sometimes kept busy for two or three days.

After all these festivities, a quiet, undisturbed life begins for the baby, — a life which is neither unpleasant nor unhealthful. It is not jolted, rocked, or trotted to sleep; it is allowed to cry if it chooses, without anybody's supposing that the world will come to an end because of its crying; and its dress is loose and easily put on, so that very little time is spent in the tiresome process of dressing and undressing. Under these conditions the baby thrives and grows strong and fat; learns to take life with some philosophy, even at a very early age; and is not subject to fits of hysterical or passionate crying, brought on by much jolting or trotting, or by the wearisome process of pinning, buttoning, tying of strings, and thrusting of arms into tight sleeves.

The Japanese baby's dress, though not as pretty as that of our babies, is in many ways much more sensible. It consists of as many wide-sleeved, straight, silk, cotton, or flannel garments as the season of the year may require, — all cut after exactly the same pattern, and that pattern the same in shape as the grown-up *kimono*. These garments are fitted, one inside of the other, before they are put on; then they are laid down on the floor and the baby is laid into them; a soft belt, attached to the outer garment or dress, is tied around the waist, and the baby is dressed without a shriek or a wail, as simply and easily as possible. The baby's dresses, like those of our babies, are made long enough to cover the little bare feet; and the sleeves cover the hands as well, so preventing the unmerciful scratching that most babies give to their faces, as well as keeping the hands warm and dry.

Babies of the lower classes, within a few weeks after birth, are carried about tied upon the back of some member of the family, frequently an older sister or brother, who is sometimes not more than five or six years old. The poorer the family, the earlier is the young baby thus put on some one's back, and one frequently sees babies not more than a month old, with bobbing heads and blinking eyes, tied by long bands of cloth to the backs of older brothers or sisters, and living in the streets in all weathers. When it is cold, the sister's *haori*, or coat, serves as an extra covering for the baby as well; and when the sun is hot, the sister's parasol keeps off its rays from the bobbing bald head. Living in public, as the Japanese babies do, they soon acquire an intelligent, interested look, and seem to enjoy the games of the elder children, upon whose backs they are carried, as much as the players themselves. Babies of the middle classes do not live in public in this way, but ride about upon the backs of their nurses until they are old enough to toddle by themselves, and they are not so often seen in the streets; as few but the poorest Japanese, even in the large cities, are unable to have a pleasant bit of garden in which the children can play and take the air. The children of the richest families, the nobility, and the imperial family, are never carried about in this way. The young child is borne in the arms of an attendant, within doors and without; but as this requires the care of some one constantly, and prevents the nurse from doing anything but care for the child, only the richest can afford this luxury. With the baby tied to her back, a woman is able to care for a child, and yet go on with her household labors, and baby watches over mother's or nurse's shoulder, between naps taken at all hours, the processes of drawing water, washing and cooking rice, and all the varied work of the house. Imperial babies are held in the arms of some one night and day, from the moment of birth until they have learned to walk, a custom which seems to render the lot of the high-born infant less comfortable in some ways than that of the plebeian child.

The flexibility of the knees, which is required for comfort in the Japanese method of sitting, is gained in very early youth by the habit of setting a baby down with its knees bent under it, instead of with its legs out straight before it, as seems to us the natural way. To the Japanese, the normal way for a baby to sit is with its knees bent under it, and so, at a very early age, the muscles and tendons of the knees are accustomed to what seems to us a most unnatural and uncomfortable posture.[1]

[1] That the position of the Japanese in sitting is really unnatural and unhygienic, is shown by recent measurements taken by the surgeons of the Japanese army.

Among the lower classes, where there are few bathing facilities in the houses, babies of a few weeks old are often taken to the public bath house and put into the hot bath. These Japanese baths are usually heated to a temperature of a hundred to a hundred and thirteen Fahrenheit, — a temperature that most foreigners visiting Japan find almost unbearable. To a baby's delicate skin, the first bath or two is usually a severe trial, but it soon becomes accustomed to the high temperature, and takes its bath, as it does everything else, placidly and in public. Born into a country where cow's milk is never used, the Japanese baby is wholly dependent upon

These measurements prove that the small stature of the Japanese is due largely to the shortness of the lower limbs, which are out of proportion to the rest of the body. The sitting from early childhood upon the legs bent at the knee, arrests the development of that part of the body, and produces an actual deformity in the whole nation. This deformity is less noticeable among the peasants, who stand and walk so much as to secure proper development of the legs; but among merchants, literary men, and others of sedentary habits, it is most plainly to be seen. The introduction of chairs and tables, as a necessary adjunct of Japanese home life, would doubtless in time alter the physique of the Japanese as a people.

its mother for milk,[1] and is not weaned entirely until it reaches the age of three or four years, and is able to live upon the ordinary food of the class to which it belongs. There is no intermediate stage of bread and milk, oatmeal and milk, gruel, or pap of some kind; for the all-important factor — milk — is absent from the bill of fare, in a land where there is neither "milk for babes" nor "strong meat for them that are full of age."

In consequence, partly, of the lack of proper nourishment after the child is too old to live wholly upon its mother's milk, and partly, perhaps, because of the poor food that the mothers, even of the higher classes, live upon, many babies in Japan are afflicted with disagreeable skin troubles, especially of the scalp and face, — troubles which usually disappear as soon as the child becomes accustomed to the regular food of the adult. Another consequence, as I imagine, of the

[1] Sometimes, in the old days, rice water was given to babies instead of milk, but it was nearly impossible to bring up a baby on this alone. Now both fresh and condensed milk are used, where the mother's milk is insufficient, but only in those parts of Japan where the foreign influence is felt.

lack of proper food at the teething period, is the early loss of the child's first teeth, which usually turn black and decay sometime before the second teeth begin to show themselves. With the exception of these two troubles, Japanese babies seem healthy, hearty, and happy to an extraordinary degree, and show that most of the conditions of their lives are wholesome. The constant out-of-door life and the healthful dress serve to make up in considerable measure for the poor food, and the Japanese baby, though small after the manner of the race, is usually plump, and of firm, hard flesh. One striking characteristic of the Japanese baby is, that at a very early age it learns to cling like a kitten to the back of whoever carries it, so that it is really difficult to drop it through carelessness, for the baby looks out for its own safety like a young monkey. The straps that tie it to the back are sufficient for safety; but the baby, from the age of one month, is dependent upon its own exertions to secure a comfortable position, and it soon learns to ride its bearer with considerable skill, instead of being merely a bundle tied to the shoulders. Any one who has ever handled a Japanese baby can testify to the amount of intelligence shown in this direction at a very early age; and this clinging with arms and legs is, perhaps, a valuable part of the training which gives to the whole nation the peculiar quickness of motion and hardness of muscle that characterize them from childhood. It is the agility and muscular quality that belong to wild animals, that we see something of in the Indian, but to a more marked degree in the Japanese, especially of the lower classes.

The Japanese baby's first lessons in walking are taken under favorable circumstances. With feet comfortably shod in the soft *tabi*, or mitten-like sock, babies can tumble about as they like, with no bump nor bruise, upon the soft matted floors of the dwelling houses. There is no furniture to fall against, and nothing about the room to render falling a thing to be feared. After learning the art of walking in the house, the baby's first attempts out of doors are hampered by the *zori* or *géta*,— a light straw sandal or small wooden clog attached to the foot by a strap passing between the toes. At the very beginning the sandal or clog is tied to the baby's foot by bits of string fastened around the ankle, but this provision for security is soon discarded, and the baby patters along like the grown people, holding on the *géta* by the strap passing between the toes. This somewhat cumbersome and inconvenient foot gear must cause many falls at first, but baby's experience in the art of balancing upon people's backs now aids in this new art of balancing upon the little wooden clogs. Babies of two or three trot about quite comfortably in *géta* that seem to give most insecure footing, and older children run, jump, hop on one foot, and play all manner of active games upon heavy clogs that would wrench our ankles and toes out of all possibility of usefulness. This foot gear, while producing an awkward, shuffling gait, has certain advantages over our own, especially for children whose feet are growing rapidly. The *géta*, even if outgrown, can never cramp the toes nor compress the ankles. If the foot is too long for the clog the heel laps over behind, but the toes do not suffer, and the use of the *géta* strengthens the ankles by affording no artificial aid or support, and giving to all the muscles of foot and leg free play, with the foot in a natural position. The toes of the Japanese retain their prehensile qualities to a surprising degree, and are used, not only for grasping the foot gear, but among mechanics almost like two supplementary hands, to aid in holding the thing worked upon. Each toe knows its work and does it, and they are not reduced to the dull uniformity of motion that characterizes the toes of a leather-shod nation. The distinction between the dress of the boy and the girl, that one notices from childhood, begins in babyhood. A very young baby wears red and yellow, but soon the boy is dressed in sober colors, — blues, grays, greens, and browns; while the little girl still wears the most gorgeous of colors and the largest of patterns in her garments, red being the predominant hue. The sex, even of a young baby, may be distinguished by the color of its clothing. White, the garb of mourning in Japan, is never used for children, but the minutest babies are dressed in bright-colored garments, and of the same materials — wadded cotton, silk, or crêpe — as those worn by adults of their social grade. As these dresses are not as easily washed as our own cambric and flannel baby clothes, there is a loss among the poorer classes in the matter of cleanliness; and the gorgeous soiled gowns are not as attractive as the more washable white garments in which our babies are dressed. For model clothing for a baby, I would suggest a combination of the Japanese style with the foreign, easily washed materials, — a combination that I have seen used in their own families by Japanese ladies educated abroad, and one in which the objections to the Japanese style of dress are entirely obviated.

The Japanese baby begins to practice the accomplishment of talking at a very early age, for its native language is singularly happy in easy expressions for children; and little babies will be heard chattering away in soft, easily spoken words long before they are able to venture alone from their perches on their mothers' or nurses' backs. A few simple words express much, and cover all wants. *Iya* expresses discontent or dislike of any kind, and is also used for "no"; *mam ma* means food; *bé bé* is the dress; *ta ta* is the sock, or house shoe, etc. We find many of the same sounds as in the baby language of English, with meanings totally different. The baby is not troubled with difficult grammatical changes, for the Japanese language has few inflections; and it is too young to be puzzled with the intricacies of the various expressions, denoting different degrees of politeness, which are the snare and the despair of the foreigner studying Japanese.

As our little girl emerges from babyhood she finds the life opening before her a bright and happy one, but one hedged about closely by the proprieties, and one in which, from babyhood to old age, she must expect to be always under the control of one of the stronger sex. Her position will be an honorable and respected one only as she learns in her youth the lesson of cheerful obedience, of pleasing manners, and of personal cleanliness and neatness. Her duties must be always either within the house, or, if she belongs to the peasant class, on the farm. There is no career or vocation open to her: she must be dependent always upon either father, husband, or son, and her greatest happiness is to be gained, not by cultivation of the intellect, but by the early acquisition of the self-control which is expected of all Japanese women to an even greater degree than of the men. This self-control must consist, not simply in the concealment of all the outward signs of any disagreeable motion, — whether of grief, anger, or pain, — but in the assumption of a cheerful smile and agreeable manner under even the most distressing of circumstances. The duty of self-restraint is taught to the little girls of the family from the tenderest years; it is their great moral lesson, and is expatiated upon at all times by their elders. The little girl must sink herself entirely, must give up always to others, must never show emotions except such as will be pleasing to those about her: this is the secret of true politeness, and must be mastered if the woman wishes to be well thought of and to lead a happy life. The effect of this teaching is seen in the attractive but dignified manners of the Japanese women, and even of the very little girls. They are not forward nor pushing, neither are they awkwardly bashful; there is no self-consciousness, neither is there any lack of *savoir faire;* a childlike simplicity is united with a womanly consideration for the comfort of those around them. A Japanese child seems to be the product of a more perfect civilization than our own, for it comes into the world with little of the savagery and barbarian bad manners that distinguish children in this country, and the first ten or fifteen years of its life do not seem to be passed in one long struggle to acquire a coating of good manners that will help to render it less obnoxious in polite society. How much of the politeness of the Japanese is the result of training, and how much is inherited from generations of civilized ancestors, it is difficult to tell; but my impression is, that babies are born into the world with a good start in the matter of manners, and that the uniformly gentle and courteous treatment that they receive from those about them, together with the continual verbal teaching of the principle of self-restraint and thoughtfulness of others, produce with very little difficulty the universally attractive manners of the people. One curious thing in a Japanese household is to see the formalities that pass between brothers and sisters, and the respect paid to age by every member of the family. The grandfather and grandmother come first of all in everything, — no one at table must be helped before them in any case; after them come the father and mother; and lastly, the children according to their ages. A younger sister must always wait for the elder and pay her due respect, even in the matter of walking into the room before her. The wishes and convenience of the elder, rather than of the younger, are to be consulted in everything, and this lesson must be learned early by children. The difference in years may be slight, but the elder-born has the first right in all cases.

Our little girl's place in the family is a pleasant one: she is the pet and plaything of father and elder brothers, and she is never saluted by any one in the family, except her parents, without the title of respect due to her position. If she is the eldest daughter, to the servants she is *O Jō Sama*, literally, young lady; to her own brothers and sisters, *Ané San*, elder sister. Should she be one of the younger ones, her given name, preceded by the honorific *O* and followed by *San*, meaning Miss, will be the name by which she will be called by younger brothers and sisters, and by the servants. As she passes from babyhood to girlhood, and from girlhood to womanhood, she is the object of much love and care and solicitude; but she does not grow up irresponsible or untrained to meet the duties which womanhood will surely bring to her. She must learn all the duties that fall upon the wife and mother of a Japanese household, as well as obtain the instruction in books and mathematics that is coming to be more and more a necessity for the women of Japan. She must take a certain responsibility in the household; must see that tea is made for the guests who may be received by her parents, — in all but the families of highest rank, must serve it herself. Indeed, it is quite the custom in families of the higher classes, should a guest, whom it is desired to receive with especial honor, dine at the house, to serve the meal, not with the family, but separately for the father and his visitor; and it is the duty of the wife or daughter, oftener the latter, to wait on them. This is in honor of the guest, not on account of the lack of servants, for there may be any number of them within call, or even in the back part of the room, ready to receive from the hands of the young girl what she has removed. She must, therefore, know the proper etiquette of the table, how to serve carefully and neatly, and, above all, have the skill to ply the *saké* bottle, so that the house may keep up its reputation for hospitality. Should guests arrive in the absence of her parents, she must receive and entertain them until the master or mistress of the house returns. She also feels a certain care about the behavior of the younger members of the family, especially in the absence of the parents. In these various ways she is trained for taking upon herself the cares of a household when the time comes. In all but the very wealthiest and most aristocratic families, the daughters of the house do a large part of the simple housework. In a house with no furniture, no carpets, no bric-à-brac, no mirrors, picture frames or glasses to be cared for, no stoves or furnaces, no windows to wash, a large part of the cooking to be done outside, and no latest styles to be imitated in clothing, the amount of work to be done by women is considerably diminished, but still there remains enough to take a good deal of time.

Every morning there are the beds to be rolled up and stored away in the closet, the mosquito nets to be taken down, the rooms to be swept, dusted, and aired before breakfast. Besides this, there is the washing and polishing of the *engawa*, or piazza, which runs around the outside of a Japanese house between the *shoji*, or paper screens that serve as windows, and the *amado*, or sliding shutters, that are closed only at night, or during heavy, driving rains. Breakfast is to be cooked and served, dishes to be washed (in cold water); and then perhaps there is marketing to be done, either at shops outside or from the vendors of fish and vegetables, who bring their huge baskets of provisions to the door; but after these duties are performed, it is possible to sit down quietly to the day's work of sewing, studying, or whatever else may suit the taste or necessities of the housewife. Of sewing there is always a good deal to be done, for many Japanese dresses must be taken to pieces whenever they are washed, and are turned, dyed, and made over again and again, so long as there is a shred of the original material left to work upon. There is washing, too, to be done, although neither with hot water nor soap; and in the place of ironing, the cotton garments, which are usually washed without ripping, must be hung up on a bamboo pole passed through the armholes, and pulled smooth and straight before they dry; and the silk, always ripped into breadths before washing, must be smoothed while wet upon a board which is set in the sun until the silk is dry.

Then there are the every day dishes which our Japanese maiden must learn to prepare. The proper boiling of rice is in itself a study. The construction of the various soups which form the staple in the Japanese bill of fare; the preparation of *mochi*, a kind of rice dough, which is prepared at the New Year, or to send to friends on various festival occasions: these and many other branches of the culinary art must be mastered before the young girl is prepared to assume the cares of married life.

But though the little girl's life is not without its duties and responsibilities, it is also not at all lacking in simple and innocent pleasures. First among the annual festivals, and bringing with it much mirth and frolic, comes the Feast of the New Year. At this time father, mother, and all older members of the family lay aside their work and their dignity, and join in the fun and sports that are characteristic of this season. Worries and anxieties are set aside with the close of the year, and the first beams of the New Year's sun bring in a season of unlimited joy for the children. For about two weeks the festival lasts, and the festal spirit remains through the whole month, prompting to fun and amusements of all kinds. From early morning until bedtime the children wear their prettiest clothes, in which they play without rebuke. Guests come and go, bringing congratulations to the family, and often gifts for all. The children's stock of toys is thus greatly increased, and the house overflows with the good things of the season, of which *mochi*, or cake made from rice dough, prepared always especially for this time, is one of the most important articles.

The children are taken with their parents to make New Year's visits to their friends and to offer them congratulations, and much they enjoy this, as, dressed in their best, they ride from house to house in *jinrikishas*.[1]

And then, during the long, happy evenings, the whole family, including even the old grandfather and grandmother, join in merry games; the servants, too, are invited to join the family party, and, without seeming forward or out of place, enter into the games with zest. One of the favorite games is "*Hyaku nin ishu*," literally "The poems of a hundred poets." It consists of two hundred cards, on each of which is printed either the first or last half of one of the hundred famous Japanese poems which give the name to the game. The poems are well known to all Japanese, of whatever sort or condition. All Japanese poems are short, containing only thirty-two syllables, and have a natural division into two parts. The one hundred cards containing the latter half of the poems are dealt and laid out in rows, face upward, before the players. One person is ap-

---

[1] *Jinrikisha*, or *kuruma*, a small, light carriage, usually with a broad top, which is drawn by a man. The *jinrikisha* is the commonest of all vehicles now in use in Japan. *Jinrikisha*-man and *kurumaya* are terms commonly used for the runner who draws the carriage.

pointed reader. To him are given the remaining hundred cards, and he reads the beginnings of the poems in whatever order they come from the shuffled pack. Skill in the game consists in remembering quickly the line following the one read, and rapidly finding the card on which it is written. Especially does the player watch his own cards, and if he finds there the end of the poem, the beginning of which has just been read, he must pick it up before any one sees it and lay it aside. If some one else spies the card first, he seizes it and gives to the careless player several cards from his own hand. Whoever first disposes of all his cards is the winner. The players usually arrange themselves in two lines down the middle of the room, and the two sides play against each other, the game not being ended until either one side or the other has disposed of all its cards. The game requires great quickness of thought and of motion, and is invaluable in giving to all young people an education in the classical poetry of their own nation, as well as being a source of great merriment and jollity among young and old.

Scattered throughout the year are various flower festivals, when, often with her whole family, our little girl visits the famous gardens where the plum, the cherry, the chrysanthemum, the iris, or the azalea attain their greatest loveliness, and spends the day out of doors in æsthetic enjoyment of the beauties of nature supplemented by art. And then there is the feast most loved in the whole year, the Feast of Dolls, when on the third day of the third month the great fire-proof storehouse gives forth its treasures of dolls, — in an old family, many of them hundreds of years old, — and for three days, with all their belongings of tiny furnishings in silver, lacquer, and porcelain, they reign supreme, arranged on red-covered shelves in the finest room of the house. Most prominent among the dolls are the effigies of the Emperor and Empress in antique court costume, seated in dignified calm, each on a lacquered dais. Near them are the figures of the five court musicians in their robes of office, each with his instrument. Beside these dolls, which are always present and form the central figures at the feast, numerous others, more plebeian, but more lovable, find places on the lower shelves, and the array of dolls' furnishings which is brought out on these occasions is something marvelous. It was my privilege to be present at the Feast of Dolls in the house of one of the *Tokugawa daimiōs*, a house in which the old forms and ceremonies were strictly observed, and over which the wave of foreign innovation had passed so slightly that even the calendar still remained unchanged, and the feast took place upon the third day of the third month of the old Japanese year, instead of on the third day of March, which is the usual time for it now. At this house, where the dolls had been accumulating for hundreds of years, five or six broad, red-covered shelves, perhaps twenty feet long or more, were completely filled with them and with their belongings. The Emperor and Empress appeared again and again, as well as the five court musicians, and the tiny furnishings and utensils were wonderfully costly and beautiful. Before each Emperor and Empress were set an elegant lacquered table service, tray, bowls, cups, *saké* pots, rice buckets, etc., all complete, and in each utensil was placed the appropriate variety of food. The *saké* used on this occasion is a sweet, white liquor, brewed especially for this feast, as different from the ordinary *saké* as sweet cider is from the hard cider upon which a man may drink himself into a state of intoxication. Besides the table service, everything that an imperial doll can be expected to need or desire is placed upon the shelves. Lacquered *norimono*, or palanquins; lacquered bullock carts, drawn by bow-legged black bulls, — these were the conveyances of the great in Old Japan, and these, in minute reproductions, are placed upon the red-covered shelves. Tiny silver and brass *hibachi*, or fire boxes, are there, with their accompanying tongs and charcoal baskets, — whole kitchens, with everything required for cooking the finest of Japanese feasts, as finely made as if for actual use, all the necessary toilet apparatus, — combs, mirrors, utensils for blackening the teeth, for shaving the eyebrows, for reddening the lips and whitening the face, — all these things are there to delight the souls of all the little girls who may have the opportunity to behold them. For three days the imperial effigies are served sumptuously at each meal, and the little girls of the family take pleasure in serving the imperial majesties; but when the feast ends, the dolls and their belongings are packed away in their boxes, and lodged in the fireproof warehouse for another year.

The Tokugawa collection, of which I have spoken, is remarkably full and costly, for it has been making for hundreds of years in one of the younger branches of a family which for two and a half centuries was possessed of almost imperial power, and lived in more than imperial luxury; but there are few households so poor that they do not from year to year accumulate a little store of toys wherewith to celebrate the feast, and, whether the toys are many or few, the feast is the event of the year in the lives of the little girls of Japan.

Beside the regular feasts at stated seasons, our little girl has a great variety of toys and games, some belonging to particular seasons, some played at any time during the year. At the New Year the popular out-of-door games are battledoor and shuttlecock, and ball. There is no prettier sight, to my mind, than a group of little girls in their many-colored wide-sleeved dresses playing with battledoor or ball. The graceful, rhythmic motion of their bodies, the bright upturned eyes, the laughing faces, are set off to perfection by the coloring of their flowing drapery; and their agility on their high, lacquered clogs is a constant source of wonder and admiration to any one who has ever made an effort to walk upon the clumsy things. There are dolls, too, that are not relegated to the storehouse when the Feast of Dolls is ended, but who are the joy and comfort of their little mothers during the whole year; and at every *kwan-ko-ba*, or bazaar, an endless variety of games, puzzles, pictures to be cut out and glued together, and amusements of all kinds, may be purchased at extremely low rates. There is no dearth of games for our little girl, and many pleasant hours are spent in the household sitting room with games, or conundrums, or stories, or the simple girlish chatter that elicits constant laughter from sheer youthful merriment.

As for fairy tales, so dear to the hearts of children in every country, the Japanese child has her full share. Often she listens, half asleep, while cuddling under the warm

CHILDHOOD. 33

quilted cover of the *kotatsu*,[1] in the cold winter evenings, to the drowsy voice of the old grandmother or nurse, who carries her away on the wings of imagination to the wonderful palace of the sea gods, or to the haunts of the terrible *oni*, monsters with red, distorted faces and fearful horns. Momotaro, the Peach Boy, with his wonderful feats in the conquest of the *oni*, is her hero, until he is supplanted by the more real ones of Japanese history.

There are occasional all-day visits to the theatre, too, where, seated on the floor in a box, railed off from those adjoining, our little girl, in company with her mother and sisters, enjoys, though with paroxysms of horror and fear, the heroic historical plays which are now almost all that is left of the heroic old Japan. Here she catches the spirit of passionate loyalty that belonged to those days, forms her ideals of what a noble Japanese woman should be willing to do for parents or husband, and comes away taught, as she could be by no other

[1] *Kotatsu*, a charcoal fire in a brazier or a small fireplace in the floor, over which a wooden frame is set and the whole covered by a quilt. The family sit about it in cold weather with the quilt drawn up over the feet and knees.

teaching, what the spirit was that animated her ancestors, — what spirit must animate her, should she wish to be a worthy descendant of the women of old.

Among these surroundings, with these duties and amusements, our little girl grows to womanhood. The unconscious and beautiful spirit of her childhood is not driven away at the dawn of womanhood by thoughts of beaux, of coming out in society, of a brief career of flirtation and conquest, and at the end as fine a marriage, either for love or money, as her imagination can picture. She takes no thought for these things herself, and her intercourse with young men, though free and unconstrained, has about it no grain of flirtation or romantic interest. When the time comes for her to marry, her father will have her meet some eligible young man, and both she and the young man will know, when they are brought together, what is the end in view, and will make up their minds about the matter. But until that time comes, the modest Japanese maiden carries on no flirtations, thinks nothing of men except as higher beings to be deferred to and waited on, and preserves the childlike innocence of manner, combined with a serene dignity under all circumstances, that is so noticeable a trait in the Japanese woman from childhood to old age.

The Japanese woman is, under this discipline, a finished product at the age of sixteen or eighteen. She is pure, sweet, and amiable, with great power of self-control, and a knowledge of what to do upon all occasions. The higher part of her nature is little developed; no great religious truths have lifted her soul above the world into a clearer and higher atmosphere; but as far as she goes, in regard to all the little things of daily life, she is bright, industrious, sweet-tempered, and attractive, and prepared to do well her duty, when that duty comes to her, as wife and mother and mistress of a household. The highest principle upon which she is taught to act is obedience, even to the point of violating all her finest feminine instincts, at the command of father or husband; and acting under that principle, she is capable of an entire self-abnegation such as few women of any race can achieve.

With the close of her childhood, the

happiest period in the life of a Japanese woman closes. The discipline that she has received so far, repressive and constant as it has often been, has been from kind and loving parents. She has freedom, to a certain degree, such as is unknown to any other country in Asia. In the home she is truly loved, often the pet and plaything of the household, though not receiving the caresses and words of endearment that children in America expect as a right, for love in Japan is undemonstrative.[1] But just at the time when her mind broadens, and the desire for knowledge and self-improvement develops, the restraints and checks upon her become more severe. Her sphere seems to grow narrower, difficulties one by one increase, and the young girl, who sees life before her as something broad and expansive, who looks to the future with expectant joy, becomes, in a few years, the weary, disheartened woman.

[1] Kisses are unknown, and regarded by conservative Japanese as an animal and disgusting way of expressing affection.

CHAPTER II.

EDUCATION.

So far we have spoken only of the domestic training of a Japanese girl. That part of her education that she gains through teachers and schools must be the subject of a separate chapter. Japan differs from most Oriental countries in the fact that her women are considered worthy of a certain amount of the culture that comes from the study of books; and although, until recently, schools for girls were unknown in the empire, nevertheless every woman, except those of the lower classes, received instruction in the ordinary written language, while some were well versed in the Chinese classics and the poetic art. These, with some musical accomplishment, an acquaintance with etiquette and the art of arranging flowers, of making the ceremonial tea, and in many cases not only of writing a beautiful hand, but of flower-painting as well, in the old days made up the whole of an ordinary woman's education. Among the lower classes, especially the merchant class, instruction was sometimes given in the various pantomimic dances which one sees most frequently presented by professional dancing girls. The art of dancing is not usually practiced by women of the higher classes, but among the daughters of the merchants special dances were learned for exhibition at home, or even at the *matsuri* or religious festival, and their performance was for the amusement of spectators, and not especially for the pleasure of the dancers themselves. These dances are modest and graceful, but from the fact that they are always learned for entertaining an audience, however small and select, and are most frequently performed by professional dancers of questionable character, the more refined and higher class Japanese do not care especially to have their daughters learn them.

In the old days, little girls were not sent to school, but, going to the house of a private teacher, received the necessary instruction in reading, and writing. The writing and reading at the beginning, are taught simultaneously, the teacher writing a letter upon a sheet of paper and telling the scholar its name, and the scholar writing it over and over until, by the time she has acquired the necessary skill in writing it, both name and form are indelibly imprinted upon her memory. To write, with a brush dipped in India ink, upon soft paper, the hand entirely without support, is an art that seldom can be acquired by a grown person, but when learned in childhood it gives great deftness in whatever other art may be subsequently studied. This is perhaps the reason why the Japanese value a good handwriting more highly than any other accomplishment, for it denotes a manual dexterity that is the secret of success in all the arts, and one who writes the Chinese characters well and rapidly can quickly learn to do anything else with the fingers.

The fault that one finds with the Japanese system — a fault that lies deeper than the mere methods of teaching, and has its root in the ideographic character of the written language — is that, while it cultivates the memory and powers of observation to a remarkable extent, and while it gives great skill in the use of the fingers, it affords little opportunity for the development of the reasoning powers.[1] The

[1] The Japanese written language is a strange combination of Chinese and Japanese, to read which a knowledge of the Chinese characters is necessary. Chinese literature written in the Chinese ideographs, which of course give no clue to the sound, are read by Japanese with the Japanese rendering of the words, and the Japanese order of words in the sentence. When there have not been exact equivalent Japanese words, a Chinese term has come into use, so that much corrupt Chinese is now well engrafted into the Japanese language, both written and spoken. In the forming of new words and technical terms Chinese words are used, as the Greek and Latin are here. There is probably no similarity in the origin of the two languages, but the Japanese borrowed from the Chinese about the sixth century A. D. their cleverly planned but most complex method of expressing thought in writing. The introduction of the Chinese literature has done much for Japan, and to master this language is one of the essentials in the education of every boy. At least seven or eight thousand characters must be learned for daily use, and there are several different styles of writing each of them. For a scholar, twice as many, or even more, must be mastered in order to read the various works in that rich literature.

The Japanese language contains a syllabary of forty-eight letters, and in books and newspapers for the common people is printed, by the side of the Chinese character, the rendering of it, in the letters of the *kana*, or Japanese alphabet.

A Japanese woman is not expected to do much in the study of Chinese. She will, of course, learn a few of the most common characters, such as are used in letter-writing, and for the rest she will read by the help of the *kana*.

years of study that are required for mastering the written language, so as to be able to grasp the thoughts already given to the world, leave comparatively little time for the conducting of any continuous thought on one's own account, and so we find in Japanese scholars — whether boys or girls — quickness of apprehension, retentive memories, industry and method in their study of their lessons, but not much originality of thought. This result comes, I believe, from the nature of the written language and the difficulties that attend the mastery of it; as a consequence of which, an educated man or woman becomes simply a student of other men's thoughts and sayings about things instead of being a student of the things themselves.

Music in Japan is an accomplishment reserved almost entirely for women, for priests, and for blind men. It seems to me quite fortunate that the musical art is not more generally practiced, as Japanese music, as a rule, is far from agreeable to the untrained ear of the outside barbarian. The *koto* is the pleasantest of the Japanese instruments, but probably on account of its large size, which makes it inconvenient to keep in a small Japanese house, it is used most among the higher classes, from the *samurai*[1] upwards. The *koto* is an embryo piano, a horizontal sounding-board, some six feet long, upon which are stretched strings supported by ivory bridges. It is played by means of ivory finger-tips fitted to the thumb, forefinger, and middle finger of each hand, and gives forth agreeable sounds, not unlike those of the harp. The player sits before the instrument on knees and heels, in the ordinary Japanese attitude, and her motions are very graceful and pretty as she touches the strings, often supplementing the strains of the instrument with her voice. The teaching of this instrument and of the *samisen*, or Japanese guitar, is almost entirely in the hands of blind men, who in Japan support themselves by the two professions of music and massage,— all the blind, who cannot learn the former, becoming adepts in the latter profession.

The arrangement of flowers is taught as

[1] The *samurai* in the feudal times were the hereditary retainers of a *daimiō*, or feudal lord. They formed the military and literary class. For further information, see chap. viii., on *Samurai Women*.

a fine art, and much time may be spent in learning how, by clipping, bending, and fixing in its place in the vase, each spray and twig may be made to look as if actually growing, for flower arranging is not merely to show the flower itself, but includes the proper arrangement of the branches, twigs, and leaves of plants. The flower plays only a small part, and is not used in decoration, except on the branch and stem as it is in nature, and the art consists in the preservation of the natural bend and growth when fixed in the vase. In every case, each branch has certain curves, which must be in harmony with the whole. Branches of pine, bamboo, and the flowering plum are much used.

Teachers spend much time in showing proper and improper combinations of different flowers, as well as the arrangement of them. Many different styles have come up, originated by the famous teachers who have founded various schools of the art, — an art which is unique and exceedingly popular, requiring artistic talent and a cultivated eye. One often sees, on going into the guest room of a Japanese house, a vase containing gracefully arranged flowers set in the *tokonoma*, or raised alcove of the room, under the solitary *kakémono* [1] that forms the chief ornament of the apartment. As these two things, the vase of flowers and the hanging scroll, are the only adornments, it is more necessary that the flowers should be carefully arranged, than in our crowded rooms, where a vase of flowers may easily escape the eye, perplexed by the multitude of objects which surround it.

The ceremonial tea must not be confounded with the ordinary serving of tea for refreshment. The proper making, and serving, and drinking of the ceremonial tea is the most formal of social observances, each step in which is prescribed by a rigid code of etiquette. The tea, instead of being the whole leaf, such as is used for ordinary occasions, is a fine, green powder. The infusion is made, not in a small pot, from which it is poured out into cups, but in a bowl, into which the hot water is poured from a dipper on to the powdered tea. The mixture is stirred with a bamboo whisk until it foams, then handed with

[1] *Kakémono*, a hanging scroll, upon which a picture is painted, or some poem or sentiment written.

much ceremony to the guest, who takes it with equal ceremony and drinks it from the bowl, emptying the receptacle at three gulps. Should there be a number of guests, tea is made for each in turn, in the order of their rank, in the same bowl. For this ceremonial tea, a special set of utensils is used, all of antique and severely simple style. The charcoal used for heating the water is of a peculiar variety; and the room in which the tea is made and served is built for that special purpose, and kept sacred for that use. This art, which is often part of the education of women of the higher classes, is taught by regular teachers, often by gentlewomen who have fallen into distressed circumstances. I remember with great vividness a visit paid to an old lady living near a provincial city of Japan, who had for years supported herself by giving lessons in this politest of arts. Her little house, of the daintiest and neatest type, seemed filled to overflowing by three foreigners, whom she received with the courtliest of welcomes. At the request of my friend, an American lady engaged in missionary work in that part of the country, she gave us a lesson in the etiquette of the tea ceremony. Every motion, from the bringing in and arranging of the utensils to the final rinsing and wiping of the tea bowl, was according to rules strictly laid down, and the whole ceremony had more the solemnity of a religious ritual than the lightness and gayety of a social occasion.

Etiquette of all kinds is not left in Japan to chance, to be learned by observation and imitation of any model that may present itself, but is taught regularly by teachers who make a specialty of it. Everything in the daily life has its rules, and the etiquette teacher has them all at her fingers' ends. There have been several famous teachers of etiquette, and they have formed systems which differ in minor points, while agreeing in the principal rules. The etiquette of bowing, the position of the body, the arms, and the head while saluting, the methods of shutting and opening the door, rising and sitting down on the floor, the manner of serving a meal, or tea, are all, with the minutest details, taught to the young girls, who, I imagine, find it rather irksome. I know two young girls of new Japan who find nothing so wearisome as their etiquette lesson, and would gladly be excused from it. I have heard them, after their teacher had left, slyly make fun of her stiff and formal manners. Such people as she will, I fear, soon belong only to the past, though it still remains to be seen how much of European manners will be engrafted on the old formalities of Japanese life. It is, perhaps, because of this regular teaching in the ways of polite society, that the Japanese girl seems never at a loss, even under unusual circumstances, but bears herself with self-possession in places where young girls in America would be embarrassed and awkward.

But the Japanese are rapidly finding out that this busy nineteenth century gives little time for learning how to shut and open doors in the politest manner, and indeed such things under the newly established school system are now relegated entirely to the girls' schools, the boys having no lessons in etiquette.

The method of teaching flower-painting is so interesting that I must speak of it before I leave the subject of accomplishments. I have said that the acquisition of skill in writing the Chinese characters was the best possible preparation for skill in all other arts. This is especially true of the art of painting, which is simply the next step, after writing has been learned. The painting master, when he comes to the house, brings no design as a model, but sits down on the floor before the little desk, and on a sheet of paper paints with great rapidity the design that he wishes the pupil to copy. It may be simply two or three blades of grass upon which the pupil makes a beginning, but she is expected to make her picture with exactly the same number of bold strokes that the master puts into his. Again and again she blunders her strokes on to a sheet of paper, until at last, when sheet after sheet has been spoiled, she begins to see some semblance of the master's copy in her own daub. She perseveres, making copy after copy, until she is able from memory to put upon the paper at a moment's notice the three blades of grass to her master's satisfaction. Only then can she go on to a new copy, and only after many such designs have been committed to memory, and the free, dashing stroke necessary for Japanese painting has been acquired, is she allowed to undertake any copying from nature, or original designing.

I have dwelt thus far only upon the entirely Japanese education that was permitted to women under the old régime. That it was an effective and refining system, all can testify who have made the acquaintance of any of the charming Japanese ladies whose schooling was finished before Commodore Perry disturbed the repose of old Japan. As I write, the image comes before me of a sweet-faced, bright-eyed little gentlewoman with whom it was my good fortune to become intimately acquainted during my stay in Tōkyō. A widow, left penniless, with one child to support, she earned the merest pittance by teaching sewing at one of the government schools in Tōkyō; but in all the circumstances of her life, narrow and busy as it needs must be, she proved herself a lady through and through. Polite, cheerful, an intelligent and cultivated reader, a thrifty housekeeper, a loving and careful mother, a true and helpful friend, her memory is associated with many of my pleasantest hours in Japan, and she is but one of the many who bear witness to the culture that might be acquired by women in the old days.

But the Japan of old is not the Japan of to-day, and in the school system now prevalent throughout the empire girls and boys are equally provided for. First the schools established by the various missionary societies, and then the government schools, offered to girls a broader education than the old instruction in Chinese, in etiquette, and in accomplishments. Now, every morning, the streets of the cities and villages are alive with boys and girls clattering along, with their books and lunch boxes in their hands, to the kindergarten, primary, grammar, high, or normal school. Every rank in life, every grade in learning, may find its proper place in the new school system, and the girls eagerly grasp their opportunities, and show themselves apt and willing students of the new learning offered to them.

By the new system, at its present stage of development, too much is expected of the Japanese boy or girl. The work required would be a burden to the quickest mind. The whole of the old education in Japanese and Chinese literature and composition — an education requiring the best years of a boy's life — is given, and grafted upon this, our common-school and high-school studies of mathematics, geography, history, and natural science. In addition to these, at all higher schools, one foreign language is required, and often two, English ranking first in the popular estimation. Many a headache do the poor, hard-working students have over the puzzling English language, in which they have to begin at the wrong end of the book and read across the page from left to right, instead of from top to bottom, and from right to left, as is natural to them. But in spite of its hard work, the new school life is cheerful and healthful, and the children enjoy it. It helps them to be really children, and, while they are young, to be merry and playful, not dignified and formal little ladies at all times. Upon the young girls, the influence of the schools is to make them more independent, self-reliant, and stronger women. In the houses of the higher classes, even now, much of the old-time system of repression is still in force. Children are indeed "seen but not heard," and from the time when they learn to walk they must learn to be polite and dignified. At school, the more progressive feeling of the times predominates among the authorities, and the children are encouraged to unbend and enjoy themselves in games and frolics, as true children should do. Much is done for the pleasure of the little ones, who often enjoy school better than home, and declare that they do not like holidays.

But the young girl, who has finished this pleasant school life, with all its advantages, is not as well fitted as under the old system for the duties and trials of married life, unless under exceptional circumstances, where the husband chosen has advanced ideas. To those teaching the young girls of Japan to-day, the problem of how to educate them aright is a deep one, and with each newly trained girl sent out go many hopes, mingled with anxieties, in regard to the training she has had as a preparation for the new life she is about to enter. The few, the pioneers, will have to suffer for the happiness and good of the many, for the problem of grafting the new on to the old is indeed a difficult one, to be solved only after many experiments.

There are many difficulties which lie in the way of the new schools that must be met, studied, and overcome. One of them is the one already referred to, the problem of how best to combine the new and the old in the school curriculum. That the old learning and literature, the old politeness and sweetness of manner, must not be given up or made little of, is evident to every right-minded student of the matter. That the newer and broader culture, with its higher morality, its greater development of the best powers of the mind, must play a large part in the Japan of the future, there is not a shadow of doubt, and the women must not be left behind in the onward movement of the nation. But how to give to the young minds the best products of the thought of two such distinct civilizations is a question that is as yet unanswered, and cannot be satisfactorily settled until the effect of the new education has begun to show itself in a generation or so of graduates from the new schools. Another difficulty is in the matter of health. Most of the new school-houses are fitted with seats and desks, such as are found in American schools. Many of them are heated by stoves or furnaces. The scholars in most cases wear the Japanese dress, which in winter is made warm enough to be worn in rooms having no artificial heat. Put this warm costume into an artificially heated room and the result is an overheating of the body, and a subsequent chill when the pupil goes, with no extra covering, into the keen out-of-door air. From this cause alone, arise many colds and lung troubles, which can be prevented when more experience has shown how the costumes of the East and West can be combined to suit the new conditions. Another part of the health problem lies in the fact that in many cases the parents do not understand the proper care of a growing girl, ambitious to excel in her studies. Instead of the regular hours, healthful food, and gentle restraint that a girl needs under those circumstances, our little Japanese maiden is allowed to sit up to any hour of the night, or arise at any hour in the morning, to prepare her lessons, is given food of most indigestible quality at all hours of the day between her regular meals, and is frequently urged to greater mental exertion than her delicate body can endure.

Another difficulty, in fitting the new school system into the customs of the people, lies in the early age at which marriages are contracted. Before the girl has finished her school course, her parents begin to wonder whether there is not danger of her being left on their hands altogether, if they do not hand her over to the first eligible young man who presents himself. Sometimes the girl makes a brave fight, and remains in school until her course is finished; more often she succumbs and is married off, bids a weeping farewell to her teachers and schoolmates, and leaves the school, to become a wife at sixteen, a mother at eighteen, and an old woman at thirty. In some cases, the breaking down of a girl's health may be traced to threats on the part of her parents that, if she does not take a certain rank in her studies, she will be taken from school and married off.

These are difficulties that may be overcome when a generation has been educated who can, as parents, avoid the mistakes that now endanger the health of a Japanese school-girl. In the mean time, boarding schools, that can attend to matters of health and hygiene among the girls, would, if they could be conducted with the proper admixture of Eastern and Western learning and manners, do a great deal toward educating that generation. The missionary schools do much in this direction, but the criticism of the Japanese upon the manners of the girls educated in missionary schools is universally severe. To a foreigner who has lived almost entirely among Japanese ladies of pure Japanese education, the manners of the girls in these schools seem brusque and awkward; and though they are many of them noble women and doing noble work, there is room for hope that in the future of Japan the charm of manner which is the distinguishing feature of the Japanese woman will not be lost by contact with our Western shortness and roughness. A happy mean undoubtedly can be reached; and when it is, the women of new Japan will be able to bear a not unfavorable comparison with the women of the old régime.

CHAPTER III.

MARRIAGE AND DIVORCE.

When the Japanese maiden arrives at the age of sixteen, or thereabouts, she is expected as a matter of course to marry. She is usually allowed her choice in regard to whether she will or will not marry a certain man, but she is expected to marry some one, and not to take too much time in making up her mind. The alternative of perpetual spinsterhood is never considered, either by herself or her parents. Marriage is as much a matter of course in a woman's life as death, and is no more to be avoided. This being the case, our young woman has only as much liberty of choice accorded to her as is likely to provide against a great amount of unhappiness in her married life. If she positively dislikes the man who is submitted to her for inspection, she is seldom forced to marry him, but no more cordial feeling than simple toleration is expected of her before marriage.

The courtship is somewhat after the following manner. A young man, who finds himself in a position to marry, speaks to some married friend, and asks him to be on the lookout for a beautiful [1] and ac-

[1] The Japanese standard of female beauty differs in many respects from our own, so that it is almost impossible for a foreigner visiting Japan to comprehend the judgments of the Japanese in regard to the beauty of their own women, and even more impossible for the untraveled Japanese to discover the reasons for a foreigner's judgments upon either Japanese or foreign beauties. To the Japanese, the ideal female face must be long and narrow; the forehead high and narrow in the middle, but widening and lowering at the sides, conforming to the outline of the beloved Fuji, the mountain that Japanese art loves to picture. The hair should be straight and glossy black, and absolutely smooth. Japanese ladies who have the misfortune to have any wave or ripple in their hair, as many of them do, are at as much pains to straighten it in the dressing as American ladies are to simulate a natural curl, when Nature has denied them that charm. The eyes should be long and narrow, slanting upward at the outer corners; and the eyebrows should be delicate lines, high above the eye itself. The distinctly aquiline nose should be low at the bridge, the curve outward beginning much lower down than upon the Caucasian face; and the eye-socket should not be outlined at all, either by the brow, the cheek, or by the nose. It is this flatness of the face about the eyes that gives the mildness of expression to all young people of Mongolian type that is so noticeable a trait always in their physiognomy. The mouth of an aristocratic Japanese lady must be small, and the lips full and red; the

complished maiden, who would be willing to become his wife. The friend, acting

neck, a conspicuous feature always when the Japanese dress is worn, should be long and slender, and gracefully curved. The complexion should be light, — a clear ivory-white, with little color in the cheeks. The blooming country girl style of beauty is not admired, and everything, even to color in the cheeks, must be sacrificed to gain the delicacy that is the *sine qua non* of the Japanese beauty. The figure should be slender, the waist long, but not especially small, and the hips narrow, to secure the best effect with the Japanese dress. The head and shoulders should be carried slightly forward, and the body should also be bent forward slightly at the waist, to secure the most womanly and aristocratic carriage. In walking, the step should be short and quick, with the toes turned in, and the foot lifted so slightly that either clog or sandal will scuff with every step. This is necessary for modesty, with the narrow skirt of the Japanese dress.

Contrast with this type the fair, curling hair, the round blue eyes, the rosy cheeks, the erect, slim-waisted, large-hipped figures of many foreign beauties, — the rapid, long, clean-stepping walk, and the air of almost masculine strength and independence, which belongs especially to English and American women, — and one can see how the Japanese find little that they recognize as beauty among them. Blue eyes, set into deep sockets, and with the bridge of the nose rising as a barrier between them, impart a fierce grotesqueness to the face, that the untraveled Japanese seldom admire. The very babies will scream with horror at first sight of a blue-eyed, light-haired foreigner, and it is only after considerable familiarity with such persons that they can be induced to show anything but the wildest fright in their presence. Foreign-

rather as advance agent, makes a canvass of all the young maidens of his acquaintance, inquiring among his friends; and finally decides that so-and-so (Miss Flower, let us say) will be a very good match for his friend. Having arrived at this decision, he goes to Miss Flower's parents and lays the case of his friend before them. Should they approve of the suitor, a party is arranged at the house of some common friend, where the young people may have a chance to meet each other and decide each upon the other's merits. Should the young folks find no fault with the match, presents are exchanged,[1] a formal betrothal is entered into, and the marriage is hastened forward. All arrangements between the contracting parties are made by go-betweens, or seconds, who hold themselves responsi-

ers who have lived a great deal among the Japanese find their standards unconsciously changing, and see, to their own surprise, that their countrywomen look ungainly, fierce, aggressive, and awkward among the small, mild, shrinking, and graceful Japanese ladies.

[1] The present from the groom is usually a piece of handsome silk, used for the *obi* or girdle. This takes the place of the conventional engagement ring of Europe and America. From the family of the bride, silk, such as is made up into men's dresses, is sent.

ble for the success of the marriage, and must be concerned in the divorce proceedings, should divorce become desirable or necessary.

The marriage ceremony, which seems to be neither religious nor legal in its nature, takes place at the house of the groom, to which the bride is carried, accompanied by her go-betweens, and, if she be of the higher classes, by her own confidential maid, who will serve her as her personal attendant in the new life in her husband's house. The trousseau and household goods, which the bride is expected to bring with her, are sent before. The household goods required by custom as a part of the outfit of every bride are as follows: A bureau; a low desk or table for writing; a work-box; two of the lacquer trays or tables on which meals are served, together with everything required for furnishing them, even to the chopsticks; and two or more complete sets of handsome bed furnishings. The trousseau will contain, if the bride be of a well-to-do family, dresses for all seasons, and handsome sashes without number; for the unchanging fashions of Japan, together with the durable quality of the dress material, make it possible for a woman, at the time of her marriage, to enter her husband's house with a supply of clothing that may last her through her lifetime. The parents of the bride, in giving up their daughter, as they do when she marries, show the estimation in which they have held her by the beauty and completeness of the trousseau with which they provide her. This is her very own; and in the event of a divorce, she brings back with her to her father's house the clothing and household goods that she carried away as a bride.

With the bride and her trousseau are sent a great number of presents from the family of the bride to the members of the groom's household. Each member of the family, from the aged grandfather to the youngest grandchild, receives some remembrance of the occasion; and even the servants and retainers, down to the *jinrikisha* men, and the *bettō* in the stables, are not forgotten by the bride's relatives. Beside this present-giving, the friends and relatives of the bride and groom, as in this country, send gifts to the young couple, often some article for use in the household, or crêpe or silk for dresses.

In old times, the wedding took place in the afternoon, but it is now usually celebrated in the evening. The ceremony consists merely in a formal drinking of the native wine (*saké*) from a two-spouted cup, which is presented to the mouths of the bride and groom alternately. This drinking from one cup is a symbol of the equal sharing of the joys and sorrows of married life. At the ceremony no one is present but the bride and bridegroom, their go-betweens, and a young girl, whose duty it is to present the cup to the lips of the contracting parties. When this is over, the wedding guests, who have been assembled in the next room during the ceremony, join the wedding party, a grand feast is spread, and much merriment ensues.[1]

On the third day after the wedding, the newly married couple are expected to make a visit to the bride's family, and for this great preparations are made. A large party is usually given by the bride's parents, either in the afternoon or evening, in honor of this occasion, to which the friends

[1] Many women still blacken their teeth after marriage, after the manner universal in the past; but this custom is, fortunately, rapidly going out of fashion.

of the bride's family are invited. The young couple bring with them presents from the groom's family to the bride's, in return for the presents sent on the wedding day.

The festivities often begin early in the afternoon and keep up until late at night. A fine dinner is served, and music and dancing, by professional performers, or some other entertainment, serve to make the time pass pleasantly. The bride appears as hostess with her mother, entertaining the company, and receiving their congratulations, and must remain to speed the last departing guest, before leaving the paternal roof.

Within the course of two or three months, the newly married couple are expected to give an entertainment, or series of entertainments, to their friends, as an announcement of the marriage. As the wedding ceremony is private, and no notice is given, nor are cards sent out, this is sometimes the first intimation that is received of the marriage by many of the acquaintances, though the news of a wedding usually travels quickly. The entertainment may be a dinner party, given at home, or at some tea-house, similar in many ways to the one given at the bride's home by her parents. Sometimes it is a garden party, and very lately it has become the fashion for officials and people of high rank to give a ball in foreign style.

Besides the entertainment, presents of red rice, or *mochi*, are sent as a token of thanks to all who have remembered the young couple. These are arranged even more elaborately than the ones sent after the birth of an heir.

The young people are not, as in this country, expected to set up housekeeping by themselves, and establish a new home. Marriages often take place early in life, even before the husband has any means of supporting a family; and as a matter of course, a son with his wife makes his abode with his parents, and forms simply a new branch of the household.

The only act required to make the marriage legal is the withdrawal of the bride's name from the list of her father's family as registered by the government, and its entry upon the register of her husband's family. From that time forward she severs all ties with her father's house, save those of affection, and is more closely related by law and custom to her husband's relatives than to her own. Even this legal recognition of her marriage is a comparatively new thing in Japan, as is any limitation of the right of divorce on the part of the husband, or extension of that right to the wife.[1]

At present in Japan the marriage relation is by no means a permanent one, as it is virtually dissoluble at the will of either party, and the condition of public opinion is such among the lower classes that it is not an unknown occurrence for a man to marry and divorce several wives in succession; and for a woman, who has been divorced once or twice, to be willing and able to marry well a second or even a third time. Among the higher classes, the dread of the scandal and gossip, that must attach themselves to troubles between man and wife, serves as a restraint upon too free use of the power of divorce; but still,

[1] "As early as 1870 an edict was published by which official notice and approbation were made necessary preliminaries to every matrimonial contract. In the following year the class-limitations upon freedom of marriage were abolished, and two years later the right of suing for a divorce was conceded to the wife." — Rein's *Japan*, p. 425.

divorces among the higher classes are so common now that one meets numerous respectable and respected persons who have at some time in their lives gone through such an experience.

One provision of the law, which serves to make most mothers endure any evil of married life rather than sue for a divorce, is the fact that the children belong to the father; and no matter how unfit a person he may be to have the care of them, the disposal of them in case of a divorce rests absolutely with him. A divorced woman returns childless to her father's house; and many women, in consequence of this law or custom, will do their best to keep the family together, working the more strenuously in this direction, the more brutal and worthless the husband proves himself to be.

The ancestor worship, as found in Japan, the tracing of relationship in the male line only, and the generally accepted belief that children inherit their qualities from their father rather than from the mother, make them his children and not hers. Thus we often see children of noble rank on the father's side, but ignoble on the mother's, inherit the rank of their father, and not permitted even to recognize their mother as in any way their equal. If she is plebeian, the children are not regarded as tainted by it.

In the case of divorce, even if the law allowed the mother to keep her children, it would be almost an impossibility for her to do so. She has no means of earning her bread and theirs, for few occupations are open to women, and she is forced to become a dependent on her father, or some male relative. Whatever they may be willing to do for her, it is quite likely that they would begrudge aid to the children of another family, with whom custom hardly recognizes any tie. The children are the children of the man whose name they bear. If the woman is a favorite daughter, it may happen that her father will take her and her children under his roof, and support them all; but this is a rare exception, and only possible when the husband first gives up all claim to the children.

There comes to my mind now a case illustrating this point, which I think I may cite without betraying confidence. It is that of a most attractive young woman who was married to a worthless husband, but lived faithfully with him for several years, and became the mother of three children. The husband, who seemed at first merely good-for-nothing, became worse as the years went by, drank himself out of situation after situation procured for him by powerful relatives, and at last became so violent that he even beat his wife and threatened his children, a proceeding most unusual on the part of a Japanese husband and father. The poor wife was at last obliged to flee from her husband's house to her mother's, taking her children with her. She sued for a divorce and obtained it, and is now married again; her youth, good looks, and high connections procuring her a very good catch for her second venture in matrimony; but her children are lost to her, and belong wholly to their worthless, drunken father.

Of the lack of permanence in the marriage relation among the lower classes, the domestic changes of one of my servants in Tōkyō afford an amusing illustration. The man, whom I had hired in the double capacity of *jinrikisha* man and *bettō* or groom, was a strong, faithful, pleasant-faced fellow, recently come to Tōkyō from the country. I inquired, when I engaged him, whether he had a wife, as I wanted some one who could remain in his room in the stable in care of the horse when he was pulling me about in the *jinrikisha*. He replied that he had a wife, but she was now at Utsunomiya, the country town from which he had come, but he would send for her at once, and she would be in Tōkyō in the course of a week or two. Two or three weeks passed and no wife appeared, so I inquired of my cook and head servant what had become of Yasaku's wife. He replied, with a twinkle in his eye, that she had found work in Utsunomiya and did not wish to come. A week more passed, and still no wife, and further inquiries elicited from the cook the information that Yasaku had divorced her for disobedience, and was on the lookout for a new and more docile helpmate. His first thought was of the maidservant of the Japanese family who lived in the same house with me, a broad-faced, red-cheeked country girl, of a very low grade of intelligence. He gave this up, however, because he thought it would not be polite to put my friends to inconvenience by taking away their servant. His next effort was by negotiation through a Tōkyō friend; but apparently Yasaku's country manners were not to the taste of the Tōkyō damsels, for he met with no success, and was at last driven to write to his father in Utsunomiya asking him to select him a wife and bring her down to Tōkyō.

The selection took a week or two, and at last my maid told me that Yasaku's wife was coming by the next morning's train. A look into the *bettō's* quarters in the stable showed great preparations for the bride. The mats, new-covered with nice straw matting, were white and clean; the *shoji* were mended with new paper; the walls covered with bright-colored pictures; and various new domestic conveniences had nearly bankrupted Yasaku, in spite of his large salary of ten dollars a month. He had ordered a fine feast at a neighboring tea house, had had cards printed with his own name in English and Japanese, and had altogether been to such great expense that he had had to put his winter clothes in pawn to secure the necessary money.

The day chosen for the marriage was rainy, and, though Yasaku spent all his time in going to trains, no bridal party appeared; and he came home at night disconsolate, to smoke his good-night pipe over his solitary *hibachi*. He was, no doubt, angry as well as disconsolate, for he sat down and penned a severe letter to his father, in which he said that, if the bride did not appear on the next day counted lucky for a wedding (no Japanese would be married on an unlucky day), they could send her back to her father's house, for he would none of her. This letter did its work, for on the next lucky day, about ten days later, the bride appeared, and Yasaku was given two days of holiday on the agreement that he should not be married again while he remained in my service. On the evening of the second day, the bride came in to pay me her respects, and, crouching on her hands and knees before me, literally trembled under the excitement of her first introduction to a foreigner. She was a girl of rather unattractive exterior, fat and heavy, and rather older than Yasaku had bargained for, I imagine; at any rate, from the first, he seemed dissatisfied with his "pig in a poke," and after a couple of months sent her home to her parents, and was all ready to start out again in the hope of better luck next time.

Here is another instance, from the woman's side. Upon one occasion, when I was visiting a Japanese lady of high rank who kept a retinue of servants, the woman who came in with the tea bowed and smiled upon me as if greeting me after a long absence. As I was in and out of the house nearly every day, I was a little surprised at this demonstration, which was quite different from the formal bow that is given by the servant to her mistress's guest upon ordinary occasions. When she went out my friend said, "You see O Kiku has come back." As I did not know that the woman had been away, the news of her return did not affect me greatly until I learned the history of her departure. It seemed that about a month before, she had left her mistress's house to be married; and the day before my visit she had quietly presented herself, and announced that she had come back, if they would take her in. My friend had asked her what had happened, — whether she had found her husband unkind. No, her husband was very nice, very kind and good, but his mother was simply unbearable; she made her work so hard that she actually had no time to rest at all. She had known before her marriage that her proposed mother-in-law was a hard task-mistress, but her husband had promised that his mother should live with his older brother, and they should have their housekeeping quite independent and separate. As the mother was then living with her older son, it seemed unlikely that she would care to move, and O Kiku San had married on that supposition. But it seemed that the wife of the older brother was both lazy and bad-tempered, and the new wife of the younger brother soon proved herself industrious and good-natured. As the mother's main thought was to go where she would get the most comfort and waiting upon, she moved from the elder son's house to that of her younger son, and began leading her new daughter-in-law such a life that she soon gave up the effort to live with her husband, sued for a divorce, obtained it, and was back in her old place, all in a month's time from the date of her marriage.

But our readers must not suppose, from the various incidents given, that few happy marriages take place in Japan, or that, in every rank of life, divorce is of every-day occurrence. On the contrary, there seems cause for wonder, not that there are so many divorces, but that there are so many happy marriages, with wives and husbands devoted and faithful. For a nobleman in the olden times to divorce his wife would have caused such a scandal and talk that it rarely occurred. If the wife were disliked, he need have little or nothing to do with her, their rooms, their meals, and their attendance being entirely separate, but he rarely took away from her the name of wife, empty as it might be. She usually would be from some other noble house, and great trouble would arise between the families if he attempted to divorce her. The *samurai* also, with the same loyalty which they displayed for their lords, were loyal to their wives, and many a novel has been written, or play acted, showing the devotion of husband and wife. The quiet, undemonstrative love, though very different from the ravings of a lover in the nineteenth century novel, is perhaps truer to life.

Among the merchants and lower classes there has been, and is, a much lower standard of morality, but the few years which have passed since the Revolution of 1868 are not a fair sample of what Japan has been. Noblemen, *samurai*, and merchants have had much to undergo in the great changes, and, as is the case in all such transition periods, old customs and restraints, and old standards of morality, have been broken down and have not been replaced. There is no doubt that men have run to excesses of all sorts, and divorces have been much more frequent of late years.

Our little Japanese maiden knows, when she blackens her teeth, dons her wedding dress, and starts on her bridal journey to her husband's house, that upon her good behavior alone depend her chances of a happy life. She is to be henceforth the property of a man of whom she probably knows little, and who has the power, at any whim, to send her back to her father's house in disgrace, deprived of her children, with nothing to live for or hope for, except that some man will overlook the disgrace of her divorce, and by marrying her give her the only opportunity that a Japanese woman can have of a home other than that of a servant or dependent. That these evils will be remedied in time, there seems little reason to doubt, but just now the various cooks who are engaged in brewing the broth of the new civilization are disagreed in regard to the condiments required for its proper flavoring. The conservatives wish to flavor strongly with the subjection and dependence of women, believing that only by that means can feminine virtue be preserved. The younger men, of foreign education, would drop into the boiling pot the flavor of culture and broader outlook; for by this means they hope to secure happier homes for all, and better mothers for their children. The missionaries and native Christians believe that, when the whole mixture is well impregnated with practical Christianity, the desired result will be achieved. All are agreed on this point, that a strong public opinion is necessary before improved legislation can produce much effect; and so, for the present, legislation remains in the background, until the time shall come when it can be used in the right way.

Let us examine the two remedies suggested by the reformers, and see what effect has been produced by each so far, and what may be expected of them in the future. Taking education first, what are the effects produced so far by educating women to a point above the old Japanese standard? In many happy homes to-day, we find husbands educated abroad, and knowing something of the home life of foreign lands, who have sought out wives of broad intellectual culture, and who make them friends and confidants, not simply housekeepers and head-servants. In such homes the wife has freedom, not such as is enjoyed by American women, perhaps, but equal to that of most European women. In such homes love and equality rule, and the power of the mother-in-law grows weak. To her is paid due respect, but she seldom has the despotic control which often makes the beginning of married life hard to the Japanese wife. These homes are sending out healthy influences that are daily having their effect, and raising the position of women in Japan.

But for the young girl whose mind has been broadened by the new education, and who marries, as the majority of Japanese girls must, not in accordance with her own wishes, but in obedience to the will of her parents, a hard life is in store. A woman's education, under the old régime, was one that fitted her well for the position that she was to occupy. The higher courses of study only serve to make her kick against the pricks, and render herself miserable where she might before have been happy. With mind and character developed by education, she may be obliged to enter the home of her husband's family, to be perhaps one among many members under the same roof. In the training of her own children, in the care of her own health and theirs, her wishes and judgment must often yield to the prejudices of those above her, under whose authority she is, and it may not be until many years have passed that she will be in a position to influence in any measure the lives of those nearest and dearest to her. Then, too, her life must be passed entirely within the home, with no opportunities to meet or to mingle with the great world of which she has read and studied. Surely her lot is harder than that of the woman of the olden time, whose plain duty always lay in the path of implicit obedience to her superiors, and who never for one moment considered obedience to the dictates of her own reason and conscience as an obligation higher than deference to the wishes of husband and parents. Education, without further amelioration of their lot as wives and mothers, can but result in making the women discontented and unhappy, — in many cases injuring their health by worry over the constant petty disappointments and baffled desires of their lives.

This to superficial observers would seem a step backward rather than forward, and it is to this cause that the present reaction against female education may be traced. The first generation or two of educated women must endure much for the sake of those who come after, and by many this vicarious suffering is misunderstood, and distaste on the part of educated girls for marriage, as it now exists in Japan, is regarded as one of the sure signs that education is a failure. Without some change in the position of wife and mother, this feeling will grow into absolute repugnance, if women continue to be educated after the Western fashion.

The second remedy that is suggested is Christianity, a remedy which is even now at work. Wherever one finds in Japan a Christian home, there one finds the wife and mother occupying the position that she occupies all over Christendom. The Christian man, in choosing his wife, feels that it is not an ordinary contract, which may be dissolved at any time at the will of the contracting parties, but that it is a union for life. Consequently, in making his choice he is more careful, takes more time, and thinks more of the personal qualities of the woman he is about to marry. Thus the chances are better at the beginning for the establishment of a happy home, and such homes form centres of influence throughout the length and breadth of the land to-day. Christianity in the future will do much to mould public sentiment in the right way, and can be trusted as a force that is sure to grow in time to be a mighty power in the councils of the nation.

One more remedy might be suggested, as a preliminary to proper legislation, or a necessary accompaniment of it, and that is, the opening of new avenues of employment for women, and especially for women of the cultivated classes. To-day marriage, no matter how distasteful, is the only opening for a woman; for she can do nothing for her own support, and cannot require her father to support her after she has reached a marriageable age. As new ways of self-support present themselves, and a woman may look forward to making a single life tolerable by her own labor, the intelligent girls of the middle class will no longer accept marriage as inevitable, but will only marry when the suitor can offer a good home, kindness, affection, and security in the tenure of these blessings. So far, there is little employment for women, except as teachers; but even this change in the condition of things is forming a class, as yet small, but increasing yearly, of women who enjoy a life of independence, though accompanied by much hard work, more than the present life of a Japanese married woman. In this class we find some of the most intelligent and respected of the women of new Japan; and the growth of this class is one of the surest signs that the present state of the laws and customs concerning marriage and divorce is so unsatisfactory to the women that it must eventually be remedied, if the educated and intelligent of the men care to take for their wives, and for the mothers of their children, any but the less educated and less intelligent of the women of their own nation.

CHAPTER IV.

WIFE AND MOTHER.

THE young wife, when she enters her husband's home, is not, as in our own country, entering upon a new life as mistress of a house, with absolute control over all of her little domain. Should her husband's parents be living, she becomes almost as their servant, and even her husband is unable to defend her from the exactions of her mother-in-law, should this new relative be inclined to make full use of the power given her by custom. Happy is the girl whose husband has no parents. Her comfort in life is materially increased by her husband's loss, for, instead of having to serve two masters, she will then have to serve only one, and that one more kind and thoughtful of her strength and comfort than the mother-in-law.

In Japan the idea of a wife's duty to her husband includes no thought of companionship on terms of equality. The wife is simply the housekeeper, the head of the establishment, to be honored by the servants because she is the one who is nearest to the master, but not for one moment to be regarded as the master's equal. She governs and directs the household, if it be a large one, and her position is one of much care and responsibility; but she is not the intimate friend of her husband, is in no sense his confidante or adviser, except in trivial affairs of the household. She appears rarely with him in public, is expected always to wait upon him and save him steps, and must bear all things from him with smiling face and agreeable manners, even to the receiving with open arms into the household some other woman, whom she knows to bear the relation of concubine to her own husband.

In return for this, she has, if she be of the higher classes, much respect and honor from those beneath her. She has, in many cases the real though often inconsiderate affection of her husband. If she be the mother of children, she is doubly honored, and if she be endowed with a good temper, good manners, and tact, she can render her position not only agreeable to herself, but one of great usefulness to those about her. It lies with her alone to make the home a pleasant one, or to make it unpleasant. Nothing is expected of the husband in this direction; he may do as he likes with his own, and no one will blame him; but if his home is not happy, even through his own folly or bad temper, the blame will fall upon his wife, who should by management do whatever is necessary to supply the deficiencies caused by her husband's shortcomings. In all things the husband goes first, the wife second. If the husband drops his fan or his handkerchief the wife picks it up. The husband is served first, the wife afterwards, and so on through the countless minutiæ of daily life. It is not the idea of the strong man considering the weak woman, saving her exertion, guarding and deferring to her; but it is the less important waiting upon the more important, the servant deferring to her master.

But though the present position of a Japanese wife is that of a dependent who owes all she has to her protector, and for whom she is bound to do all she can in return, the dependence is in many cases a happy one. The wife's position, especially if she be the mother of children, is often pleasant, and her chief joy and pride lies in the proper conduct of her house and the training of her children. The service of her parents-in-law, however, must remain her first duty during their lifetime. She must make it her care to see that they are waited upon and served with what they like at meals, that their clothes are carefully and nicely made, and that countless little attentions are heaped upon them. As long as her mother-in-law lives, the latter is the real ruler of the house; and though in many cases the elder lady prefers freedom from responsibility to the personal superintendence of the details of housekeeping, she will not hesitate to require of her daughter-in-law that the house be kept to her satisfaction. If the maiden's lot is to be the first daughter-in-law in a large family, she becomes simply the one of the family from whom the most drudgery is expected, who obtains the fewest favors, and who is expected to have always the pleasantest of tempers under circumstances not altogether conducive to repose of spirit. The wife of the oldest son has, however, the advantage that, when her mother-in-law dies or retires, she becomes the mistress of the house and the head lady of the family, a position for which her apprenticeship to the old lady has probably exceptionally well fitted her.

Next to her parents-in-law, her duty is to her husband. She must herself render to him the little services that a European expects of his valet. She must not only take care of his clothing, but must bring it to him and help him put it on, and must put away with care whatever he has taken off; and she often takes pride in doing with her own hands many acts of service which might be left to servants, and which are not actually demanded of her, unless she has no one under her to do them. In the poorer families all the washing, sewing, and mending that is required is always done by the wife; and even the Empress herself is not exempt from these duties of personal service, but must wait upon her husband in various ways.

When the earliest beams of the sun shine in at the cracks of the dark wooden shutters which surround the house at night, the young wife in the family softly

WIFE AND MOTHER. 89

arises, puts out the feeble light of the *andon*,[1] which has burned all night, and, quietly opening one of the sliding doors, admits enough light to make her own toilet. She dresses hastily, only putting a few touches here and there to her elaborate coiffure, which she has not taken down for her night's rest.[2] Next she goes to arouse the servants, if they are not already up, and with them prepares the modest breakfast. When the little lacquer tables, with rice bowls, plates, and chopsticks are arranged in place, she goes softly to see whether her parents and husband are awake, and if they have hot water, charcoal fire, and whatever else they may need for their toilet. Then with her own hands,

[1] The *andon* is the standing lamp, inclosed in a paper case, used as a night lamp in all Japanese houses. Until the introduction of kerosene lamps, the *andon* was the only light used in Japanese houses. The light is produced by a pith wick floating in a saucer of vegetable oil.

[2] The pillow used by ladies is merely a wooden rest for the head, that supports the neck, leaving the elaborate head-dress undisturbed. The hair is dressed by a professional hair-dresser, who comes to the house once in two or three days. In some parts of Japan, as in Kiōto, where the hair is even more elaborately dressed than in Tōkyō, it is much less frequently arranged. The process takes two hours at least.

or with the help of the servants, she slides back the wooden shutters, opening the whole house to the fresh morning air and sunlight. It is she, also, who directs the washing and wiping of the polished floors, and the folding and putting away of the bedding, so that all is in readiness before the morning meal.

When breakfast is over, the husband starts for his place of business, and the little wife is in waiting to send him off with her sweetest smile and her lowest bow, after having seen that his foot-gear — whether sandal, clog, or shoe — is at the door ready for him to put on, his umbrella, book, or bundle at hand, and his *kuruma* waiting for him.

Certainly a Japanese man is lucky in having all the little things in his life attended to by his thoughtful wife, — a good, considerate, careful body-servant, always on hand to bear for him the trifling worries and cares. There is no wonder that there are no bachelors in Japan. To some degree, I am sure, the men appreciate these attentions; for they often become much in love with their sweet, helpful wives, though they do not share with them the greater things of life, the ambitions and the hopes of men.

The husband started on his daily rounds, the wife settles down to the work of the house. Her sphere is within her home, and though, unlike other Asiatic women, she goes without restraint alone through the streets, she does not concern herself with the great world, nor is she occupied with such a round of social duties as fill the lives of society women in this country. Yet she is not barred out from all intercourse with the outer world, for there are sometimes great dinner parties, given perhaps at home, when she must appear as hostess, side by side with her husband, and share with him the duty of entertaining the guests. There are, besides, smaller gatherings of friends of her husband, when she must see that the proper refreshments are served, if they be only the omnipresent tea and cake. She may, perhaps, join in the number and listen to the conversation; but if there are no ladies, she will probably not appear, except to attend to the wants of her guests. There are also lady visitors — friends and relatives — who come to make calls, oftentimes from a distance, and nearly always unexpectedly, whose entertainment devolves on the wife. Owing to the great distances in many of the cities, and the difficulties that used to attend going from place to place, it has become a custom not to make frequent visits, but long ones at long intervals. A guest often stays several hours, remaining to lunch or dinner, as the case may be, and, should the distance be great, may spend the night. So rigid are the requirements of Japanese hospitality that no guest is ever allowed to leave a house without having been pressed to partake of food, if it be only tea and cake. Even tradesmen or messengers who come to the house must be offered tea, and if carpenters, gardeners, or workmen of any kind are employed about the house, tea must be served in the middle of the afternoon with a light lunch, and tea sent out to them often during their day's work. If a guest arrives in *jinrikisha*, not only the guest, but the *jinrikisha* men must be supplied with refreshments. All these things involve much thought and care on the part of the lady of the house.

In the homes of rich and influential men of wide acquaintance, there is a great deal going on to make a pleasant variety for the ladies of the household, even although the variety involves extra work and responsibility. The mistress of such a household sees and hears a great deal of life; and her position requires no little wisdom and tact, even where the housewife has the assistance of good servants, capable, as many are, of sharing not only the work, but the responsibility as well. Clever wives in such homes see and learn much, in an indirect way, of the outside world in which the men live; and may become, if they possess the natural capabilities for the work, wise advisers and sympathizers with their husbands in many things far beyond their ordinary field of action. An intelligent woman, with a strong will, has often been, unseen and unknown, a mighty influence in Japan. That her power for good or bad, outside of her influence as wife and mother, is a recognized fact, is seen in the circumstance that in novels and plays women are frequently brought in as factors in political plots and organized rebellions, as well as in acts of private revenge.

Still the life of the average woman is a

quiet one, with little to interrupt the monotony of her days with their never-ending round of duties; and to the most secluded homes only an occasional guest comes to enliven the dull hours. The principal occupation of the wife, outside of her housekeeping and the little duties of personal service to husband and parents, is needlework. Every Japanese woman (excepting those of the highest rank) knows how to sew, and makes not only her own garments and those of her children, but her husband's as well. Sewing is one of the essentials in the education of a Japanese girl, and from childhood the cutting and putting together of crêpe, silk, and cotton is a familiar occupation to her. Though Japanese garments seem very simple, custom requires that each stitch and seam be placed in just such a way; and this way is something of a task to learn. To the uninitiated foreigner, the general effect of the loosely worn *kimono* is the same, whether the garment be well or ill made; but the skillful seamstress can easily discover that this seam is not turned just as it should be, or that those stitches are too long or too short, or carelessly or unevenly set.

Fancy work[1] or embroidery is not done in the house, the gorgeous embroidered Japanese robes being the product of professional workmen. Instead of the endless fancy work with silks, crewels, or worsteds, over which so many American ladies spend their leisure hours, many of the Japanese ladies, even of the highest rank, devote much time to the cultivation of the silkworm. In country homes, and in the great cities as well, wherever spacious grounds afford room for the growth of mulberry trees, silkworms are raised and watched with care; an employment giving much pleasure to those engaged in it.

It is difficult for any one who has not experimented in this direction to realize how tender these little spinners are. If a strong breeze blow upon them, they are likely to suffer for it, and the least change in the atmosphere must be guarded against. For forty days they must be carefully watched, and the great, shallow, bamboo basket trays containing them changed almost daily. New leaves for their food

---

[1] The one exception to this statement, so far as I know, is the species of silk mosaic made by the ladies in the *daimiôs'* houses. (See chap. vii.)

must be given frequently, and as the least dampness might be fatal, each leaf, in case of rainy weather, is carefully wiped. Then, too, the different ages of the worms must be considered in preparing their food; as, for the young worms, the leaves should be cut up, while for the older ones it is better to serve them whole. When, finally, the buzzing noise of the crunching leaves has ceased, and the last worm has put himself to sleep in his precious white cocoon, the work of the ladies is ended; for the cocoons are sent to women especially skilled in the work, by them to be spun off, and the thread afterwards woven into the desired fabric. When at last the silk, woven and dyed, is returned to the ladies by whose care the worms were nourished until their work was done, it is shown with great pride as the product of the year's labor, and if given as a present will be highly prized by the recipient.

Among the daily tasks of the housewife, one, and by no means the least of her duties, is to receive, duly acknowledge, and return in suitable manner, the presents received in the family. Presents are not confined to special seasons, although upon certain occasions etiquette is rigid in its requirements in this matter, but they may be given and received at all times, for the Japanese are preëminently a present-giving nation. For every present received, sooner or later, a proper return must be sent, appropriate to the season and to the rank of the receiver, and neatly arranged in the manner that etiquette prescribes. Presents are not necessarily elaborate; callers bring fruit of the season, cake, or any delicacy, and a visit to a sick person must be accompanied by something appropriate. Children visiting in the family are always given toys, and for this purpose a stock is kept on hand. The present-giving culminates at the close of the year, when all friends and acquaintances exchange gifts of more or less value, according to their feelings and means. Should there be any one who has been especially kind, and to whom return should be made, this is the time to do so.

Tradesmen send presents to their patrons, scholars to teachers, patients to their physicians, and, in short, it is the time when all obligations and debts are paid off, in one way or another. On the seventh day of the seventh month, there is another general interchange of presents, although not so universal as at the New Year. It can easily be imagined that all this present-giving entails much care, especially in families of influence; and it must be attended to personally by the wife, who, in the secret recesses of her storeroom, skillfully manages to rearrange the gifts received, so that those not needed in the house may be sent, not back to their givers, but to some place where a present is due. The passing-on of the presents is an economy not of course acknowledged, but frequently practiced even in the best families, as it saves much of the otherwise ruinous expense of this custom.

As time passes by, occasional visits are paid by the young wife to her own parents or to other relatives. At stated times, too, she, and others of the family, will visit the tombs of her husband's ancestors, or of her own parents, if they are no longer living, to make offerings and prayers at the graves, to place fresh branches of the *sakaki* [1] before the tombs, and to see that

[1] *Sakaki*, the *Cleyera Japonica*, a sacred plant emblematic of purity, and much used at funerals and in the decoration of graves.

the priests in charge of the cemetery have attended to all the little things which the Japanese believe to be required by the spirits of the dead. Even these visits are often looked forward to as enlivening the monotony of the humdrum home life. Sometimes all the members of the family go together on a pleasure excursion, spending the day out of doors, in beautiful gardens, when some one of the much-loved flowers of the nation is in its glory; and the little wife may join in this pleasure with the rest, but more often she is the one who remains at home to keep the house in the absence of others. The theatre, too, a source of great amusement to Japanese ladies, is often a pleasure reserved for a time later in life.

The Japanese mother takes great delight and comfort in her children, and her constant thought and care is the right direction of their habits and manners. She seems to govern them entirely by gentle admonition, and the severest chiding that is given them is always in a pleasant voice, and accompanied by a smiling face. No matter how many servants there may be, the mother's influence is always direct and personal. No thick walls and long passageways separate the nursery from the grown people's apartments, but the thin paper partitions make it possible for the mother to know always what her children are doing, and whether they are good and gentle with their nurses, or irritable and passionate. The children never leave the house, nor return to it, without going to their mother's room, and there making the little bows and repeating the customary phrases used upon such occasions. In the same way, when the mother goes out, all the servants and the children escort her to the door; and when her attendant shouts "*O kaeri,*" which is the signal of her return, children and servants hasten to the gate to greet her, and do what they can to help her from her conveyance and make her home-coming pleasant and restful.

The father has little to do with the training of his children, which is left almost entirely to the mother, and, except for the interference of the mother-in-law, she has her own way in their training, until they are long past childhood. The children are taught to look to the father

WIFE AND MOTHER. 101

as the head, and to respect and obey him as the one to whom all must defer; but the mother comes next, almost as high in their estimation, and, if not so much feared and respected, certainly enjoys a larger share of their love.

The Japanese mother's life is one of perfect devotion to her children; she is their willing slave. Her days are spent in caring for them, her evenings in watching over them; and she spares neither time nor trouble in doing anything for their comfort and pleasure. In sickness,[1] in health, day and night, the little ones are her one thought; and from the home of the noble to the humble cot of the peasant, this tender mother-love may be seen in all its different phases. The Japanese woman has so few on whom to lavish her affection, so little to live for beside her children, and no hopes in the future except through them, that it is no wonder that

---

[1] Since the introduction of the foreign system of medicine and nursing, the Japanese realize so acutely the lack of conveniences and appliances for nursing the sick in their own homes, that cases of severe or even serious illness are usually sent to hospitals, where the invalids can have the comforts that even the wealthy Japanese homes cannot furnish.

she devotes her life to their care and service, deeming the drudgery that custom requires of her for them the easiest of all her duties. Even with plenty of servants, the mother performs for her children nearly all the duties often delegated to nurses in this country. Mother and babe are rarely separated, night or day, during the first few years of the baby's life, and the mother denies herself any entertainment or journey from home when the baby cannot accompany her. To give the husband any share in the baby-work would be an unheard-of thing, and a disgrace to the wife; for in public and in private the baby is the mother's sole charge, and the husband is never asked to sit up all night with a sick baby, or to mind it in any way at all. Nothing in all one's study of Japanese life seems more beautiful and admirable than the influence of the mother over her children, — an influence that is gentle and all-pervading, bringing out all that is sweetest and noblest in the feminine character, and affording the one almost unlimited opportunity of a Japanese woman's life. The lot of a childless wife in Japan is a sad one. Not only is she denied the hopes and the pleasures of a mother in her children, but she is an object of pity to her friends, and well does she know that Confucius has laid down the law that a man is justified in divorcing a childless wife. All feel that through her, innocent though she is, the line has ceased; that her duty is unfulfilled; and that, though the name be given to adopted sons, there is no heir of the blood. A man rarely sends away his wife solely with this excuse, but children are the strongest of the ties which bind together husband and wife, and the childless wife is far less sure of pleasing her husband. In many cases she tries to make good her deficiencies by her care of adopted children; in them she often finds the love which fills the void in her heart and home, and she receives from them in after-life the respect and care which is the crown of old age.

We have hitherto spoken of married life when the wife is received into her husband's home. Another interesting side of Japanese marriage is when a man enters the wife's family, taking her name and becoming entirely one of her family, as usually the wife becomes of the husband's. When there are daughters but no sons in a family to inherit the name, one of three things may happen: a son may be adopted early in life and grow up as heir; or he may be adopted with the idea of marrying one of the daughters; or, again, no one may have been formally adopted, but on the eldest daughter's coming to a marriageable age, her family and friends seek for her a *yoshii*, that is to say, some man (usually a younger son) who is willing and able to give up his family name, and, by marrying the daughter, become a member of her family and heir to the name. He cuts off all ties from his own family, and becomes a member of hers, and the young couple are expected to live with her parents. In this case the tables are turned, and it is he who has to dread the mother-in-law; it is his turn to have to please his new relatives and to do all he can to be agreeable. He, too, may be sent away and divorced by the all-powerful parents, if he does not please; and such divorces are not uncommon. Of course, in such marriages, the woman has the greater power, and the man has to remember what he owes her;

and though the woman yields to him obediently in all respects, it is an obedience not demanded by the husband, as under other circumstances. In such marriages the children belong to the family whose name they bear, so that in case of divorce they remain in the wife's family, unless some special arrangement is made about them.

It may be wondered why young men ever care to enter a family as *yoshii*. There is only one answer,—it is the attraction of wealth and rank, very rarely that of the daughter herself. In the houses of rich *daimiōs* without sons, *yoshii* are very common, and there are many younger sons of the nobility, themselves of high birth, but without prospects, who are glad enough to become great lords. In feudal times, the number of *samurai* families was limited. Several sons of one family could not establish different *samurai* families, but all but the eldest son, if they formed separate houses, must enroll themselves among the ranks of the common people. Hence the younger sons were often adopted into other *samurai* families as *yoshii*, where it was desired to secure a succession to a name that must otherwise die out. Since the Restoration, and the breaking down of the old class distinctions, young men care more for independence than for their rank as *samurai;* and it is now quite difficult to find *yoshii* to enter *samurai* families, unless it be because of the attractiveness and beauty of the young lady herself. Many a young girl who could easily make a good marriage with some suitable husband, could she enter his family, is now obliged to take some inferior man as *yoshii*, because few men in these days are willing to change their names, give up their independence, and take upon themselves the support of aged parents-in-law; for this also is expected of the *yoshii*, unless the family that he enters is a wealthy one.

From this custom of *yoshii*, and its effect upon the wife's position, we see that, in certain cases, Japanese women are treated as equal with men. It is not because of their sex that they are looked down upon and held in subjection, but it is because of their almost universal dependence of position. The men have the right of inheritance, the education, habits of self-reliance, and are the bread-winners. Wherever the tables are turned, and the men are dependents of the women, and even where the women are independent of the men, — there we find the relations of men to women vastly changed. The women of Japan must know how to do some definite work in the world beyond the work of the home, so that their position will not be one of entire dependence upon father, husband, or son. If fathers divided their estates between sons and daughters alike, and women were given, before the law, right to hold property in their own names, much would be accomplished towards securing them in their positions as wives and mothers; and divorce, the great evil of Japanese home life to-day, would become simply a last resort to preserve the purity of the home, as it is in most civilized countries now.

The difference between the women of the lower and those of the higher classes, in the matter of equality with their husbands, is quite noticeable. The wife of the peasant or merchant is much nearer to her husband's level than is the wife of the Emperor. Apparently, each step in the social scale is a little higher for the man than it is for the woman, and lifts him a little farther above his wife. The peasant and his wife work side by side in the field, put their shoulders to the same wheel, eat together in the same room, at the same time, and whichever of them happens to be the stronger in character governs the house, without regard to sex. There is no great gulf fixed between them, and there is frequently a consideration for the wife shown by husbands of the lower class, that is not unlike what we see in our own country. I remember the case of a *jinrikisha* man employed by a friend of mine in Tōkyō, who was much laughed at by his friends because he actually used to spend some of his leisure moments in drawing the water required for his household from a well some distance away, and carrying the heavy buckets to the house, in order to save the strength of his little, delicate wife. That cases of such devotion are rare is no doubt true, but that they occur shows that there is here and there a recognition of the claims that feminine weakness has upon masculine strength.

A frequent sight in the morning, in Tōkyō, is a cart heavily laden with wood, charcoal, or some other country produce, creaking slowly along the streets, propelled by a farmer and his family. Sometimes one will see an old man, his son, and his son's wife with a baby on her back, all pushing or pulling with might and main; the woman with tucked-up skirts and tight-fitting blue trousers, a blue towel enveloping her head, — only to be distinguished from the men by her smaller size and the baby tied to her back. But when evening comes, and the load of produce has been disposed of, the woman and baby are seen seated upon the cart, while the two men pull it back to their home in some neighboring village. Here, again, is the recognition of the law that governs the position of woman in this country, — the theory, not of inferior position, but of inferior strength; and the sight of the women riding back in the empty carts at night, drawn by their husbands, is the thing that strikes a student of Japanese domestic life as nearest to the customs of our own civilization in regard to the relations of husbands and wives.

Throughout the country districts, where the women have a large share in the labor that is directly productive of wealth, where they not only work in the rice fields, pick the tea crops, gather the harvests, and help draw them to market, but where they have their own productive industries, such as caring for the silkworms, and spinning, and weaving both silk and cotton, we find the conventional distance between the sexes much diminished by the important character of feminine labor; but in the cities, and among the classes who are largely either indirect producers or non-producers, the only labor of the women is that personal service which we account as menial. It is for this reason, perhaps, that the gap widens as we go upward in society, and between the same social levels as we go cityward.

The wife of the countryman, though she may work harder and grow old earlier, is more free and independent than her city sister; and the wife of the peasant, pushing her produce to market, is in some ways happier and more considered than the wife of the noble, who must spend her life among her ladies-in-waiting, in the seclusion of her great house with its beautiful garden, the plaything of her husband in his leisure hours, but never his equal, or the sharer of his cares or of his thoughts.

One of the causes which must be mentioned as contributing to the lowering of the wife's position, among the higher and more wealthy classes, lies in the system of concubinage which custom allows, and the law until quite recently has not discouraged. From the Emperor, who was, by the old Chinese code of morals, allowed twelve supplementary wives, to the *samurai,* who are permitted two, the men of the higher classes are allowed to introduce into their families these *mékaké,* who, while beneath the wife in position, are frequently more beloved by the husband than the wife herself. It must be said, however, to the credit of many husbands, that in spite of this privilege, which custom allows, there are many men of the old school who are faithful to one wife, and never introduce this discordant element into the household. Even should he keep *mékaké,* it is often unknown to the wife, and she is placed in a separate establishment of her own. And in spite of the code of morals requiring submission in any case on the part of the woman, there are many wives of the *samurai* and lower classes who have enough spirit and wit to prevent their husbands from ever introducing a rival under the same roof. In this way the practice is made better than the theory.

Not so with the more helpless wife of the nobleman, for wealth and leisure make temptation greater for the husband. She submits unquestioningly to the custom requiring that the wife treat these women with all civility. Their children she may even have to adopt as her own. The lot of the *mékaké* herself is rendered the less endurable, from the American point of view, by the fact that, should the father of her child decide to make it his heir, the mother is thenceforth no more to it than any other of the servants of the household. For instance, suppose a hitherto childless noble is presented with a son by one of his concubines, and he decides by legal adoption to make that son his heir: the child at its birth, or as soon afterwards as is practicable, is taken from its mother and placed in other hands, and the mother never sees her own child until, on the thirtieth day after its birth, she goes with the other servants of the household to pay her respects to her young master. If it were not for the habit of abject obedience to parents which Japanese custom has exalted into the one feminine virtue, few women could be found of respectable families who would take a position so devoid of either honor or satisfaction of any kind as that of *mékaké*. That these positions are not sought after must be said, to the honor of Japanese womanhood. A nobleman may obtain *samurai* women for his "*O mékaké*" (literally, honorable concubines), but they are never respected by their own class for taking such positions. In the same way the *mékaké* of *samurai* are usually from the *héimin*. No woman who has any chance of a better lot will ever take the unenviable position of *mékaké*.

A law which has recently been promulgated strikes at the root of this evil, and, if enforced, will in course of time go far toward extirpating it. Henceforth in Japan, no child of a concubine, or of adoption from any source, can inherit a noble title. The heir to the throne must hereafter be the son, not only of the Emperor, but of the Empress, or the succession passes to some collateral branch of the family. This law does not apply to Prince Haru, the present heir to the throne, as, although he is not the son of the Empress, he was legally adopted before the promulgation of the law; but should he die, it will apply to all future heirs.

That public opinion is moving in the right direction is shown by the fact that the young men of the higher classes do not care to marry the daughters of *mékaké*, be they ever so legally adopted by their own fathers. When the girls born of such unions become a drug in the matrimonial market, and the boys are unable to keep up the succession, the *mékaké* will go out of fashion, and the real wife will once more assume her proper importance.[1]

Upon the 11th day of February, 1889, the day on which the Emperor, by his own act in giving a constitution to the people, limited his own power for the sake of putting his nation upon a level with the most civilized nations of the earth, he at the

[1] It is worth while to mention in this connection the noteworthy efforts made by the Woman's Christian Temperance Union of Japan in calling the attention of the public to this custom, and in arousing public sentiment in favor of legislation against not only this system, but against the licensed houses of prostitution. Though there has not yet been any practical result, much discussion has ensued in the newspapers and magazines, lectures have been given, and much strong feeling aroused, which may, before long, produce radical change.

same time, and for the first time, publicly placed his wife upon his own level. In an imperial progress made through the streets of Tōkyō, the Emperor and Empress, for the first time in the history of Japan, rode together in the imperial coach. Until then, the Emperor, attended by his chief gentlemen-in-waiting and his guards, had always headed the procession, while the Empress must follow at a distance with her own attendants. That this act on the part of the Emperor signifies the beginning of a new and better era for the women of Japan, we cannot but hope; for until the position of the wife and mother in Japan is improved and made secure, little permanence can be expected in the progress of the nation toward what is best and highest in the Western civilization. Better laws, broader education for the women, a change in public opinion on the subject, caused by the study, by the men educated abroad, of the homes of Europe and America, — these are the forces which alone can bring the women of Japan up to that place in the home which their intellectual and moral qualities fit them to fill. That Japan is infinitely ahead of other Oriental countries in her practices in this matter is greatly to her credit; but that she is far behind the civilized nations of Europe and America, not only in practice but in theory, is a fact that is incontestable, and a fact that, unless changed, must sooner or later be a stumbling-block in the path of her progress toward the highest civilization of which she is capable.[1] The European practice cannot be grafted upon the Asiatic theory, but the change in the home must be a radical one, to secure permanent good results. As long as the wife has no rights which the husband is bound to respect, no great advance

[1] Many of the thinking men of Japan, though fully recognizing the injustice of the present position of woman in society, and the necessity of reform in the marriage and divorce laws, refuse to see the importance of any movement to change them. Their excuse is, that such power in the hands of the husband over his wife might be abused, but that in fact it is not. Wrongs and injustice are rare, they argue, and kind treatment, affection, and even respect for the wife is the general rule; and that the keeping of the power in the hands of the husband is better than giving too much freedom to women who are without education. These men wish to wait until every woman is educated, before acting in a reform movement, while many conservatives oppose the new system of education for girls as making them unwomanly. Between these two parties, the few who really wish for a change are utterly unable to act.

can be made, for human nature is too mean and selfish to give in all cases to those who are entirely unprotected by law, and entirely unable to protect themselves, those things which the moral nature declares to be their due. In the old slave times in the South, many of the negroes were better fed, better cared for, and happier than they are to-day; but they were nevertheless at the mercy of men who too often thought only of themselves, and not of the human bodies and souls over which they had unlimited power. It was a condition of things that could not be prevented by educating the masters so as to induce them to be kind to their slaves; it was a condition that was wrong in theory, and so could not be righted in practice. In the same way the position of the Japanese wife is wrong in theory, and can never be righted until legislation has given to her rights which it still denies. Education will but aggravate the trouble to a point beyond endurance. The giving to the wife power to obtain a divorce will not help much, but simply tend to weaken still further the marriage tie. Nothing can help surely and permanently but the growth of a sound public opinion, in regard to the position of the wife, that will, sooner or later, have its effect upon the laws of the country. Legislation once effected, all the rest will come, and the wife, secure in her home and her children, will be at the point where her new education can be of use to her in the administration of her domestic affairs and the training of her children; and where she will finally become the friend and companion of her husband, instead of his mere waitress, seamstress, and housekeeper, — the plaything of his leisure moments, too often the victim of his caprices.

CHAPTER V.

OLD AGE.

No Japanese woman is ashamed to show that she is getting along in years, but all take pains that every detail of the dress and coiffure shall show the full age of the wearer. The baby girl is dressed in the brightest of colors and the largest of patterns, and looks like a gay butterfly or tropical bird. As she grows older, colors become quieter, figures smaller, stripes narrower, until in old age she becomes a little gray moth or plain-colored sparrow. By the sophisticated eye, a woman's age can be told with considerable accuracy by the various little things about her costume,[1] and no woman cares to appear

[1] Children wear their hair on top of their heads while very young, and the manner of arranging it is one of the distinctive marks of the age of the child. The *marumagi*, the style of headdress of married ladies, consisting of a large puff of hair on the top of the head, diminishes in size with the age of the wearer until, at sixty or seventy, it is not more than a few inches in width. The number, size, and variety of ornamental hairpins, and the tortoise-shell comb worn in front, all vary with the age.

younger than her real age, or hesitates to tell with entire frankness the number of years that have passed over her head.

The reason for this lies, at least in part, in the fact that every woman looks forward to the period of old age as the time when she will attain freedom from her life-long service to those about her, — will be in the position of adviser of her sons, and director of her daughters-in-law; will be a person of much consideration in the family, privileged to amuse herself in various ways, to speak her own mind on most subjects, and to be waited upon and cared for by children and grandchildren, in return for her long years of faithful service in the household. Should her sight and other bodily powers remain good, she will doubtless perform many light tasks for the general good, will seldom sit idle by herself, but will help about the sewing and mending, the marketing, shopping, housework, and care of the babies, tell stories to her grandchildren after their lessons are learned, give the benefit of her years of experience to the young people who are still bearing the heat and burden of the day, and, by her prayers and visits to the temple at stated seasons, will secure the favor of the gods for the whole family, as well as make her own preparations for entry into the great unknown toward which she is rapidly drifting. Is there wonder that the young wife, steering her course with difficulty among the many shoals and whirlpools of early married life, looks forward with anticipation to the period of comparative rest and security that comes at the end of the voyage? As she bears all things, endures all things, suffers long, and is kind, as she serves her mother-in-law, manages her husband's household, cares for her babies, the thought that cheers and encourages her in her busy and not too happy life is the thought of the sunny calm of old age, when she can lay her burdens and cares on younger shoulders, and bask in the warmth and sunshine which this Indian Summer of her life will bring to her.

In the code of morals of the Japanese, obedience to father, husband, or son is exalted into the chief womanly virtue, but the obedience and respect of children, both male and female, to their parents, also occupies a prominent position in their ethical system. Hence, in this latter stage of a woman's career, the obedience expected of her is often only nominal, and in any case is not so absolute and unquestioning as that of the early period; and the consideration and respect that a son is bound to show to his mother necessitates a care of her comfort, and a consultation of her wishes, that renders her position one of much greater freedom than can be obtained by any woman earlier in life. She has, besides, reached an age when she is not expected to remain at home, and she may go out into the streets, to the theatre, or other shows, without the least restraint or fear of losing her dignity.

A Japanese woman loses her beauty early. At thirty-five her fresh color is usually entirely gone, her eyes have begun to sink a little in their sockets, her youthful roundness and symmetry of figure have given place to an absolute leanness, her abundant black hair has grown thin, and much care and anxiety have given her face a pathetic expression of quiet endurance. One seldom sees a face that indicates a soured temper or a cross disposition, but the lines that show themselves as the years go by are lines that indicate suffering and disappointment, patiently and sweetly borne. The lips never forget to smile; the voice remains always cheerful and sympathetic, never grows peevish and worried, as is too often the case with overworked or disappointed women in this country. But youth with its hopeful outlook, its plans and its ambitions, gives way to age with its peaceful waiting for the end, with only a brief struggle for its place; and the woman of thirty-five is just at the point when she has bid good-by to her youth, and, having little to hope for in her middle life, is doing her work faithfully, and looking forward to an old age of privilege and authority, the mistress of her son's house, and the ruler of the little domain of home.

But I have spoken so far only of those happy women whose sons grow to maturity, and who manage to evade the dangerous reefs of divorce upon which so many lives are shipwrecked. What becomes of the hundreds who have no children to rise up and call them blessed, but who have in old age to live as dependents upon their brothers or nephews? Even these, who in this country often lead hard and unrewarded lives of toil among their happier relatives, find in old age a pleasanter lot than that of youth. Many such old ladies I have met, whose short hair or shaven heads proclaim to all who see them that the sorrow of widowhood has taken from them the joy that falls to other women, but whose cheerful, wrinkled faces and happy, childlike ways have given one a feeling of pleasure that the sorrow is past, and peace and rest have come to their declining years. Fulfilling what little household tasks they can, respected and self-respecting members of the household, the *O Bă San*, or Aunty, is not far removed in the honor and affection of the children from the *O Bā San*, or Grandma, but both alike find a peaceful shelter in the homes of those nearest and dearest to them.

One of the happiest old ladies I have ever seen was one who had had a rough and stormy life. The mother of many children, most of whom had died in infancy, she was at last left childless and a widow. In her children's death the last tie that bound her to her husband's family was broken, and, rather than be a burden to them, she made her home for many years with her own younger brother, taking up again the many cares and duties of a mother's life in sharing with the mother the bringing up of a large family of children. One by one, from the oldest to the youngest, each has learned to love the old aunty, to be lulled asleep on her back, and to go to her in trouble when mother's hands were too full of work. Many the caress received, the drives and walks enjoyed in her company, the toys and candies that came out unexpectedly from the depths of mysterious drawers, to comfort many an hour of childish grief. That was years ago, and the old aunty's hard times are nearly over. Hale and hearty at threescore years and ten, she has seen these children grow up one by one, until now some have gone to new homes of their own. Her bent form and wrinkled face are ever welcome to her children, — hers by the right of years of patient care and toil for them. They now, in their turn, enjoy giving her pleasure, and return to her all the love she has lavished upon them. It is a joy to see her childlike pride and confidence in them all, and to know that they have filled the place left vacant by the dead with whom had died all her hopes of earthly happiness.

The old women of Japan, — how their withered faces, bent frames, and shrunken, yellow hands abide in one's memory! One seldom sees among them what we would call beauty, for the almost universal shrinking with age that takes place among the Japanese covers the face with multitudinous wrinkles, and produces the effect of a withered russet apple; for the skin, which in youth is usually brightened by red cheeks and glossy black hair, in old age, when color leaves cheek and hair, has a curiously yellow and parchment-like look. But with all their wrinkles and ugliness, there is a peculiar charm about the old women of Japan.

In Tōkyō, when the grass grows long upon your lawn, and you send to the gardener to come and cut it, no boy with patent lawn-mower, nor stalwart countryman with scythe and sickle, answers your summons, but some morning you awake to find your lawn covered with old women. The much-washed cotton garments are faded to a light blue, the exact match of the light blue cotton towels in which their heads are swathed, and on hands and knees, each armed with an enormous pair of shears, the old ladies clip and chatter cheerfully all day long, until the lawn is as smooth as velvet under their careful cutting. An occasional rest under a tree, for pipes and tea, is the time for much cheerful talk and gossip; but the work, though done slowly and with due attention to the comfort of the worker, is well done, and certainly accomplished as rapidly as any one could expect of laborers who earn only from eight to twelve cents a day. Another employment for this same class of laborers is the picking of moss and grass from the crevices of the great walls that inclose the moats and embankments of the capital. Mounted on little ladders, they pick and scrape with knives until the wall is clear and fresh, with no insidious growth to push the great uncemented stones out of their places.

In contrast with these humble but cheerful toilers may be mentioned another class of women, often met with in the great cities. Dressed in rags and with covered heads and faces, they wander about the streets playing the *samisen* outside the latticed windows, and singing with cracked voices some wailing melody. As they go from house to house, gaining a miserable pittance by their weird music, they seem the embodiment of all that is hopeless and broken-hearted. What they are or whence they come, I know not, but they always remind me of the grasshopper in the fable, who danced and sang through the brief summer, to come, wailing and wretched, seeking aid from her thriftier neighbor when at last the winter closed in upon her.

As one rides about the streets, one often sees a little, white-haired old woman trotting about with a yoke over her shoulders from which are suspended two swinging baskets, filled with fresh vegetables. The fact that her hair is still growing to its natural length shows that she is still a wife and not a widow; her worn and patched blue cotton clothes, bleached light from much washing, show that extreme poverty is her lot in life; and as she hobbles along with the gait peculiar to those who carry a yoke, my thoughts are busy with her home, which, though poor and small, is doubtless clean and comfortable, but my eye follows her through the city's crowd, where laborer, soldier, student, and high official jostle each other by the way. Suddenly I see her pause before the gateway of a temple. She sets her burden down, and there in the midst of the bustling throng, with bowed head, folded hands, and moving lips, she invokes her god, snatching this moment from her busy life to seek a blessing for herself and her dear ones. The throng moves busily on, making a little eddy around the burden she has laid down, but paying no heed to the devout little figure standing there; then in a moment the prayer is finished; she stoops, picks up her yoke, balances it on her shoulders, and moves on with the crowd, to do her share while her strength lasts, and to be cared for tenderly, I doubt not, by children and children's children when her work is done.

Another picture comes to me, too, a picture of one whose memory is an inspiring thought to the many who have the honor to call her "mother." A stately old lady, left a widow many years ago, before the recent changes had wrought havoc preparatory to further progress, she seemed always to me the model of a mother of the old school. Herself a woman of thorough classical education, her example and teaching were to both sons and daughters a constant inspiration; and in her old age she found herself the honored head of a family well known in the arts of war and peace, a goodly company of sons and daughters, every one of them heirs of her spirit and of her intellect. Though conservative herself, and always clinging to the old customs, she put no block in the path of her children's progress, and her fine character, heroic spirit, and stanch loyalty to what she believed were worth more to her children than anything else could have been. Tried by war, by siege, by banishment, by danger and sufferings of all kinds, to her was given at last an old age of prosperity among children of whom she might well be proud. Keeping her physical vigor to the end, and dying at last, after an illness of only two days, her spirit passed out into the great unknown, ready to meet its dangers as bravely as she had met those of earth, or to enjoy its rest as sweetly and appreciatively as she had enjoyed that of her old age in the house of her oldest son.

My acquaintance with her was limited by our lack of common language, but was a most admiring and appreciative one on my side; and I esteem it one of the chief honors of my stay in Japan, that upon my last meeting with her, two weeks before her death, she gave me her wrinkled but still beautiful and delicately shaped hand at parting, — a deference to foreign customs that she only paid upon special occasions.

Two weeks later, amid such rain as Japanese skies know all too well how to let fall, I attended her funeral at the cemetery of Aoyama. The cemetery chapel was crowded, but a place was reserved for me, on account of special ties that bound me to the family, just behind the long line of white-robed mourners. In the Buddhist faith she had lived, and by the Buddhist ceremonial she was buried, — the chanted ritual, the gorgeously robed priests, and the heavy smell of incense in the air reminding one of a Roman Catholic ceremony. The white wooden coffin was placed upon a bier at the entrance to the chapel, and when the priests had done their work, and the ecclesiastical ceremony was over, the relatives arose, one by one, walked over to the coffin, bowed low before it, and placed a grain of incense upon the little censer that stood on a table before the bier, then, bowing again, retired to their places. Slowly and solemnly, from the tall soldier son, his hair already streaked with gray, to the two-year-old grandchild, all paid this last token of respect to a noble spirit; and after the relatives the guests, each in the order of rank or nearness to the deceased, stepped forward and performed the same ceremony before leaving the room. What the meaning of the rite was, I did not know, whether a worship of strange gods or no; but to me, as I performed the act, it only signified the honor in which I held the memory of a heroic woman who had done well her part in the world according to the light that God had given her.

Japanese art loves to picture the old woman with her kindly, wrinkled face, leaving out no wrinkle of them all, but giving with equal truthfulness the charm of expression that one finds in them. Long life is desired by all as passionately as by ancient Hebrew poet and psalmist, and with good reason, for only by long life can a woman attain the greatest honor and happiness. We often exclaim in impatience at the thought of the weakness and dependence of old age, and pray that we may die in the fullness of our powers, before the decay of advancing years has made us a burden upon our friends. But in Japan, dependence is the lot of woman, and the dependence of old age is that which is most respected and considered. An aged parent is never a burden, is treated by all with the greatest love and tenderness; and if times are hard, and food and other comforts are scarce, the children, as a matter of course, deprive themselves and their children to give ungrudgingly to their old father and mother. Faults there are many in the Japanese social system, but ingratitude to parents, or disrespect to the aged, must not be named among them; and Young America may learn a salutary lesson by the study of the place that old people occupy in the home.

It is not only for the women of Japan, but for the men as well, that old age is a time of peace and happiness. When a man reaches the age of fifty or thereabouts, often while apparently in the height of his vigor, he gives up his work or business and retires, leaving all the property and income to the care of his eldest son, upon whom he becomes entirely dependent for his support.[1] This support is never begrudged him, for the care of parents by their children is as much a matter of course in Japan as the care of children by those who give them birth. A man thus rarely makes provision for the future, and looks with scorn on foreign customs which seem to betoken a fear lest, in old age, ungrateful children may neglect their parents and cast them aside. The feeling, so strong in America, that dependence is of itself irksome and a thing to be dreaded, is altogether strange to the Japanese mind. The married son does not care to take his wife to a new and independent home of his own, and to support her and her children by his own labor or on his own income, but he takes her to his father's house, and thinks it no shame that his family live upon his parents. But in return, when the parents wish to retire from active life, the son takes upon himself ungrudgingly the burden of

[1] It is this custom of going into early retirement that made it possible for the nobles in old times to keep the Emperor always a child. The ruling Emperor would be induced to retire from the throne at the age of sixteen or twenty; thus making room for some baby, who would be in his turn the puppet of his ambitious courtiers.

their support, and the bread of dependence is never bitter to the parents' lips, for it is given freely. To the time-honored European belief, that a young man must be independent and enterprising in early life in order to lay by for old age, the Japanese will answer that children in Japan are taught to love their parents rather than ease and luxury, and that care for the future is not the necessity that it is in Europe and America, where money is above everything else, — even filial love. This habit of thought may account for the utter want of provision for the future, and the disregard for things pertaining to the accumulation of wealth, which often strikes curiously the foreigner in Japan. A Japanese considers his provision for the future made when he has brought up and educated for usefulness a large family of children. He invests his capital in their support and education, secure of bountiful returns in their gratitude and care for his old age. It is hard for the men of old Japan to understand the rush and struggle for riches in America, — a struggle that too often leaves not a pause for rest or quiet pleasure until sickness or death overtakes the indefatigable worker. The *go inkyo*[1] of Japan is glad enough to lay down early in life the cares of the world, to have a few years of calm and peace, undisturbed by responsibilities or cares for outside matters. If he be an artist or a poet, he may, uninterrupted, spend his days with his beloved art. If he is fond of the ceremonial tea, he has whole afternoons that he may devote to this æsthetic repast; and even if he has none of these higher tastes, he will always have congenial friends who are ready to share the *saké* bottle, to join in a quiet smoke over the *hibachi*, or to play the deep-engrossing game of *go*, or *shogi*, the Japanese chess. To the Japanese mind, to be in the company of a few kindred souls, to spend the long hours of a summer's afternoon at the ceremonial tea party, sipping tea and conversing in a leisurely manner on various subjects, is an enjoyment second to none. A cultivated Japanese of the old times must receive an education fitting him especially

[1] *Go Inkyo Sama* is the title belonging to a retired old gentleman or old lady. *Inkyo* is the name of the house or suite of rooms set apart for such a person, and the title itself is made up of this word with the Chinese honorific *go* and the title *Sama*, the same as *San*, used in addressing all persons except inferiors.

for such pursuits. At these meetings of friends, artistically or poetically inclined, the time is spent in making poems and exchanging wittily turned sentiments, to be read, commented on, and responded to; or in the making of drawings, with a few bold strokes of the brush, in illustration of some subject given out. Such enjoyments as these, the Japanese believe, cannot be appreciated or even understood by the practical, rush-ahead American, the product of the wonderful but material civilization of the West.

Thus, amid enjoyments and easy labors suited to their closing years, the elder couple spend their days with the young people, cared for and protected by them. Sometimes there will be a separate suite of rooms provided for them; sometimes a little house away from the noises of the household, and separated from the main building by a well-kept little garden. In any case, as long as they live they will spend their days in quiet and peace; and it is to this haven, the *inkyo,* that all Japanese look forward, as to the time when they may carry out their own inclinations and tastes with an income provided for the rest of their days.

CHAPTER VI.

COURT LIFE.

THE court of the Emperor was, in the early ages of Japan, the centre of whatever culture and refinement the country could boast, and the emperors themselves took an active part in the promotion of civilization. The earliest history of Japan is so wrapped in the mists of legend and tradition that only here and there do we get glimpses of heroic figures, — leaders in those early days. Demigods they seem, children of Heaven, receiving from Heaven by special revelation the wisdom or strength by means of which they conquered their enemies, or gave to their subjects new arts and better laws. The traditional emperors, the early descendants of the great Jimmu Tenno,[1] seem to have been merely conquer-

[1] The Japanese claim for their present Emperor direct descent from Jimmu Tenno, the Son of the Gods; and it is for this reason that the Emperor is supposed to be divine, and the representative of the gods on the earth.

ing chieftains, who by virtue of their descent were regarded as divine, but who lived the simple, hardy life of the savage king, surrounded by wives and concubines, done homage to by armed retainers and subject chiefs, but living in rude huts, and moving in and out among the soldiers, not in the least retired into the mysterious solitude which in later days enveloped the Son of the Gods. The first emperors ruled not only by divine right, but by personal force and valor; and the stories of the valiant deeds of these early rulers kept strong the faith of the people in the divine qualities of the imperial house during the hundreds of years when the Emperor was a mere puppet in the hands of ambitious and powerful nobles.

Towards the end of this legendary period, a figure comes into view that for heroic qualities cannot be excelled in the annals of any nation, — Jingu Kōgō, the conqueror

The dynasty, for about twenty-five hundred years since Jimmu Tenno, has never been broken. It must, however, be said in connection with this statement, that the Japanese family is a much looser organization than that known to our Western civilization, on account of the customs of concubinage and adoption, and that descent through family lines is not necessarily actual descent by blood.

of Corea, who alone, among the nine female rulers of Japan, has made an era in the national history. She seems to have been from the beginning, like Jeanne D'Arc, a hearer of divine voices; and through her was conveyed to her unbelieving husband a divine command, to take ship and sail westward to the conquest of an unknown land. Her husband questioned the authenticity of the message, took the earthly and practical view that, as there was no land to be seen in the westward, there could be no land there, and refused to organize any expedition in fulfillment of the command; but for his unbelief was sternly told that he should never see the land, but that his wife should conquer it for the son whom she should bear after the father's death. This message from the gods was fulfilled. The Emperor died in battle shortly after, and the Empress, after suppressing the rebellion in which her husband had been killed, proceeded to organize an expedition for the conquest of the unknown land beyond the western sea. By as many signs as those required by Gideon to assure himself of his divine mission, the Empress tested the call that had come to her, but at last, satisfied that the voices were from Heaven, she gave her orders for the collection of troops and the building of a navy. I quote from Griffis the inspiring words with which she addressed her generals: "The safety or destruction of our country depends upon this enterprise. I intrust the details to you. It will be your fault if they are not carried out. I am a woman and young. I shall disguise myself as a man, and undertake this gallant expedition, trusting to the gods and to my troops and captains. We shall acquire a wealthy country. The glory is yours, if we succeed; if we fail, the guilt and disgrace shall be mine." What wonder that her captains responded to such an appeal, and that the work of recruiting and shipbuilding began with a will! It was a long preparation that was required — sometimes, to the impatient woman, it seemed unnecessarily slow — but by continual prayer and offerings she appealed to the gods for aid; and at last all was ready, and the brave array of ships set sail for the unknown shore, the Empress feeling within her the new inspiration of hope for her babe as yet unborn. Heaven smiled upon them from the start. The clearest of skies, the most favoring of breezes, the smoothest of seas, favored the god-sent expedition; and tradition says that even the fishes swarmed in shoals about their keels, and carried them on to their desired haven. The fleet ran safely across to southern Corea, but instead of finding battles and struggles awaiting them, the king of the country met them on the beach to receive and tender allegiance to the invaders, whose unexpected appearance from the unexplored East had led the natives to believe that their gods had forsaken them. The expedition returned laden with vast wealth, not the spoil of battle, but the peaceful tribute of a bloodless victory; and from that time forward Japan, through Corea, and later by direct contact with China itself, began to receive and assimilate the civilization, arts, and religions of China. Thus through a woman Japan received the start along the line of progress which made her what she is to-day, for the sequel of Jingu Kōgō's Corean expedition was the introduction of almost everything which we regard as peculiar to civilized countries. With characteristic belittling of the woman and exalting of the man, the whole martial career of the

Empress is ascribed to the influence of her son as yet unborn, — a son who by his valor and prowess has secured for his deified spirit the position of God of War in the Japanese pantheon. We should say that pre-natal influences and heredity produced the heroic son; the Japanese reason from the other end, and show that all the noble qualities of the mother were produced by the influence of the unborn babe.

With the introduction of literature, art, and Buddhism, a change took place in the relations of the court to the people. About the Emperor's throne there gathered not only soldiers and governors, but the learned, the accomplished, the witty, the artistic, who found in the Emperor and the court nobles munificent patrons by whom they were supported, and before whom they laid whatever pearls they were able to produce. The new culture sought not the clash of arms and the shout of soldiers, but the quiet and refinement of palaces and gardens far removed from the noise and clamor of the world. And while emperors sought to encourage the new learning and civilization, and to soften the warlike qualities of the people about them, there was a frontier along which the savages still made raids into the territory which the Japanese had wrested from them, and which it required a strong arm and a quick hand to guard for the defense of the people. But the Emperor gradually gave up the personal leadership in war, and passed the duty of defending the nation into the hands of one or another of the great noble families. The nobles were not by any means slow to see the advantage to be gained for themselves by the possession of the military power in an age when might made right, even more than it does to-day, and when force, used judiciously and with proper deference to the prejudices of the people, could be made to give to its possessor power even over the Emperor himself. And so gradually, in the pursuit of the new culture and the new religion, the emperors withdrew themselves more and more into seclusion, and the court became a little world in itself,— a centre of culture and refinement into which few excitements of war or politics ever came. While the great nobles wrangled for the possession of the power, schemed and fought and turned the nation upside down; while the heroes of the country rose, lived, fought, and died, — the Emperor, amid his ladies and his courtiers, his priests and his literary men, spent his life in a world of his own; thinking more of this pair of bright eyes, that new and charming poem, the other witty saying of those about him, than of the kingdom that he ruled by divine right; and retiring, after ten years or so of puppet kinghood, from the seclusion of his court to the deeper seclusion of some Buddhist monastery.

Within the sacred precincts of the court, much time was given to such games and pastimes as were not too rude or noisy for the refinement that the new culture brought with it. Polo, football, hunting with falcons, archery, etc., were exercises not unworthy of even the most refined of gentlemen, and certain noble families were trained hereditarily in the execution of certain stately, antique dances, many of them of Chinese or Corean origin. The ladies, in trailing garments and with flowing hair, reaching often below the knees, played a not inconspicuous part, not only because of their beauty and grace, but for their quickness of wit, their learning in the classics, their skill in repartee, and their quaint fancies, which they embodied in poetic form.[1]

Much attention was given to that harmony of art with nature that the Japanese taste makes the *sine qua non* of all true artistic effort. The gorgeously embroidered gowns must change with the changing season, so that the cherry succeeds the plum, the wistaria the cherry, and so on through the whole calendar of flowers, upon the silken robes of the court, as regularly as in the garden that graces the palace grounds. And so with the confectionery, which in Japan is made in dainty imitation of flowers and fruits. The chrysanthemum blooms in sugar no earlier than

---

[1] In ancient times, before the long civil wars of the Middle Ages, much attention was given by both men and women to poetry, and many of the classics of Japanese literature are the works of women. Among these distinguished writers can be mentioned Murasaki Shikibu, Seishō Nagon, and Iséno Taiyu, all court ladies in the time of the Emperor Ichijō (about 1000 A. D.). The court at that time was the centre of learning, and much encouragement was given by the Emperor to literary pursuits, the cultivation of poetry, and music. The Emperor gathered around him talented men and women, but the great works that remain are, strange to say, mostly those of women.

on its own stalk; the little golden orange, with its dark green leaves, is on the confectioner's list in winter, when the real orange is yellow on its tree. The very decorations of the palace must be changed with the changing of the months; and *kakémono* and vase are alternately stored in the *kura* and brought out to decorate the room, according as their designs seem in harmony with the mood of Nature. This effort to harmonize Nature and Art is seen to-day, not only in the splendid furnishings of the court, but all through the decorative art of Japan. In every house the decorations are changed to suit the changing seasons.

Through the years when Japan was adopting the civilization of China, a danger threatened the nation, — the same danger that threatens it to-day: it was the danger lest the adoption of so much that was foreign should result in a servile copying of all that was not Japanese, and lest the introduction of literature, art, and numerous hitherto unknown luxuries should take from the people their independence, patriotism, and manliness. But this result was happily avoided; and at a time when the language was in danger of being swept almost out of existence by the introduction of Chinese learning through Chinese letters, the women of Japan, not only in their homes and conversation, but in the poetry and lighter literature of the country, preserved a strain of pure and graceful Japanese, and produced some of the standard works of a distinctly national literature. Favor at court to-day, as in the olden times, is the reward, not of mere rank, beauty, and grace of person, but must be obtained through the same intellectual endowments, polished by years of education, that made so many women famous in the mediæval history of Japan. Many court ladies have read much of their national literature, so that they are able to appreciate the *bonmots* which contain allusions in many cases to old poems, or plays on words; and are able to write and present to others, at fitting times, those graceful but untranslatable turns of phrase which form the bulk of Japanese poetry.[1] Even

---

[1] The court ladies in immediate contact with the Emperor and Empress are selected from the daughters of the nobles. Only in the present reign have a few samurai women risen to high positions at court on account of special talents.

in this busy era of Méiji,[1] the Emperor and his court keep up the old-time customs, and strive to promote a love of the beautiful poetry of Japan. At each New Year some subject appropriate to the time is chosen and publicly announced. Poems may be written upon this subject by any one in the whole realm, and may be sent to the palace before a certain date fixed as the time for closing the list of competitors. All the poems thus sent are examined by competent judges, who select the best five and send them to the Emperor, an honor more desired by the writers than the most favorable of reviews or the largest of emoluments are desired by American poets. Many of the other poems are published in the newspapers. It is interesting to note that many of the prominent men and women of the country are known as competitors, and that many of the court ladies join in the contest.

There are also, at the palace, frequent meetings of the poets and lovers of poetry

[1] *Méiji* (Enlightened Rule) is the name of the era that began with the present Emperor's accession to the throne. The year A. D. 1890 is the twenty-third year of Méiji, and would be so designated in all Japanese dates.

connected with the court. At these meetings poems are composed for the entertainment of the Emperor and Empress, as well as for the amusement of the poets themselves.

In the school recently established for the daughters of the nobles, under the charge of the imperial household, much attention is given to the work of thoroughly grounding the scholars in the Japanese language and literature, and also to making them skillful in the art of composing poetry. At the head of the school, in the highest position held by any woman in the employ of the government, is a former court lady, who is second to none in the kingdom, not only in her knowledge of all that belongs to court etiquette, but in her study of the history and literature of her own people, and in her skill in the composition of these dainty poems. A year or two ago, when one of the scholars in the school died after a brief decline, her schoolmates, teachers, and school friends wrote poems upon her death, which they sent to the bereaved parents.

It is difficult for any Japanese, much more so for a foreigner, to penetrate into the seclusion of the palace and see anything of the life there, except what is shown to the public in the occasional entertainments given at court, such as formal receptions and dinner parties. In 1889, the new palace, built on the site of the old Tokugawa Castle, burnt seventeen years ago, was finally completed; and it was my privilege to see, before the removal of the court, not only the grand reception rooms, throne-room, and dining-room, but also the private apartments of the Emperor and Empress. The palace is built in Japanese style, surrounded by the old castle moats, but there are many foreign additions to the palace and grounds. It is heated and lighted in foreign style, and the larger rooms are all furnished after the magnificent manner of European palaces; while the lacquer work, carvings, and gorgeous paneled ceilings remind one of the finest of Japanese temples. The private apartments of the Emperor and Empress are, on the other hand, most simple, and in thorough Japanese style; and though the woodwork and polished floors of the corridors are very beautiful, the paintings and lacquer work most exquisite, there is little in this simplicity to denote the abode of royalty. It seems that their majesties, though outwardly conforming to many European customs, and to the European manner of dress, prefer to live in Japanese ways, on matted, not carpeted floors, reposing on them rather than on chairs and beds.

Their apartments are not large; each suite consisting of three rooms opening out of each other, the Empress's rooms being slightly smaller than the Emperor's, and those of the young Prince Haru, the heir apparent, again a little smaller. The young prince has a residence of his own, and it is only on his visits that he occupies his apartments in his father's palace. There are also rooms for the Empress dowager to occupy on her occasional visits. All of these apartments are quite close together in one part of the palace, and are connected by halls; but the private rooms of the court ladies are in an entirely separate place, quite removed, and only connected with the main building by a long, narrow passageway, running through the garden. There, in the rooms assigned to them, each one has her own private establishment, where she stays when she is not on duty in attendance on the Emperor and Empress. Each lady has her own servants, and sometimes a younger sister or a dependent may be living there with her, though they are entirely separate from the court and the life there, and must never be seen in any of the other parts of the building. In these rooms, which are like little homes in themselves, cooking and housekeeping are done, entirely independent of the other parts of the great palace; and the tradesmen find their way through some back gate to these little establishments, supplying them with all the necessaries of life, as well as the luxuries.

A court lady is a personage of distinction, and lives in comparative ease and luxury, with plenty of servants to do all the necessary work. Besides her salary, which of course varies with the rank and the duties performed, but is always liberal enough to cover the necessary expenses of dress, the court lady receives many presents from the Emperor and Empress, which make her position one of much luxury.

The etiquette of the imperial household

is very complicated and very strict, though many of the formalities of the olden times have been given up. The court ladies are models of conservatism. In order to be trained for the life there and its duties, they usually enter the court while mere children of ten or eleven, and serve apprenticeship to the older members. In the rigid seclusion of the palace they are strictly, almost severely, brought up, and trained in all the details of court etiquette. Cut off from all outside influences while young, the little court maidens are taught to go through an endless round of formalities which they are made to think indispensable. These details of etiquette extend not only to all that concerns the imperial household, but to curious customs among themselves, and in regard to their own habits. Many of these ideas have come down from one generation to another, within the narrow limits of the court, so that the life there is a curious world in itself, and very unlike that in ordinary Japanese homes.

But among all the ladies of Japan to-day, — charming, intellectual, refined, and lovely as many of them are, — there is no one nobler, more accomplished, more beautiful in life and character, than the Empress herself. The Emperor of Japan, though he may have many concubines, may have but one wife, and she must be chosen out of one of the five highest noble families.[1] Haru Ko, of the noble family of Ichijō, became Empress in the year 1868, one year after her husband, then a boy of seventeen, had ascended the throne, and the very year of the overthrow of the Shōgunate,[2] and the restoration of the Em-

[1] The Empresses of Japan are not chosen from any branch of the imperial family, but from among the daughters of the five of the great *kugé*, or court nobles, who are next in rank to the imperial princes. The choice usually rests with the Emperor or his advisers, and would be naturally given to the most worthy, whether in beauty or accomplishments. No doubt one reason why the Empress is regarded as far below the Emperor is, that she is not of royal blood, but one of the subjects of the Empire. In the old times, the daughters of the Emperor could never marry, as all men were far beneath them in rank. These usually devoted their lives to religion, and as Shintō priestesses or Buddhist nuns dwelt in the retirement of temple courts or the seclusion of cloisters.

[2] Tokugawa Shōguns were the military rulers of the Tokugawa family, who held the power in Japan for a period of two hundred and fifty years. They are better known to Americans, perhaps, under the title of *Tycoon* (Great Prince), a name assumed, or rather revived, to im-

peror to actual power and the leading part in the government. Reared amid the deep and scholarly seclusion of the old court at Kyōto, the young Empress found herself occupying a position very different from that for which she had been educated, — a position the duties and responsibilities of which grow more multifarious as the years go by. Instead of a life of rigid seclusion, unseeing and unseen, the Empress has had to go forth into the world, finding there the pleasures as well as the duties of actual leadership. With the removal of the court to Tōkyō, and the reappearance of the Emperor, in bodily form, before his people, there came new opportunities for the Empress, and nobly has she used them. From the time when, in 1871, she gave audience to the five little girls of the samurai class who were just setting forth on a journey to America, there to study and fit themselves to play a part in the Japan of the future, on through twenty years of change

press the foreigners when Commodore Perry was negotiating in regard to treaties. The Shōgun held the daimiōs in forced subjection, — a subjection that was shaken in 1862, and broken at last in the year 1868, when, by the fall of the Shōgunate, the Emperor was restored to direct power over his people.

and progress, the Empress Haru Ko has done all that lay within her power to advance the women of her country. Many stories are afloat which show the lovable character of the woman, and which have given her an abiding place in the affections of the people.

Some years ago, when the castle in Tōkyō was burned, and the Emperor and Empress were obliged to take refuge in an old daimiō's house, a place entirely lacking in luxuries and considerably out of repair, some one expressed to her the grief that all her people felt, that she should have to put up with so many inconveniences. Her response was a graceful little poem, in which she said that it mattered little how she was situated, as long as she was sure of a home in the hearts of her people. That home, which fire can never consume, she has undoubtedly made for herself.

Upon another occasion, when Prince Iwakura, one of the leaders of Japan in the early days of the crisis through which the country is still passing, lay dying at his home, the Empress sent him word that she was coming to visit him. The prince, afraid that he could not do honor to such a guest, sent her word back that he was very ill, and unable to make proper preparation to entertain an Empress. To this the Empress replied that he need make no preparations for her, for she was coming, not as an Empress, but as the daughter of Ichijō, his old friend and colleague, and as such he could receive her. And then, setting aside imperial state and etiquette, she visited the dying statesman, and brightened his last hours with the thought of how lovely a woman stood as an example before the women of his beloved country.

Many of the charities and schools of new Japan are under the Empress's special patronage; and this does not mean simply that she allows her name to be used in connection with them, but it means that she thinks of them, studies them, asks questions about them, and even practices little economies that she may have the more money to give to them. There is a charity hospital in Tōkyō, having in connection with it a training school for nurses, that is one of the special objects of her care. Last year she gave to it, at the end of the year, the savings from her own private allowance, and concerning this act an editorial from the "Japan Mail" speaks as follows: —

"The life of the Empress of Japan is an unvarying routine of faithful duty-doing and earnest charity. The public, indeed, hears with a certain listless indifference, engendered by habit, that her Majesty has visited this school, or gone round the wards at that hospital. Such incidents all seem to fall naturally into the routine of the imperial day's work. Yet to the Empress the weariness of long hours spent in class-rooms or in laboratories, or by the beds of the sick, must soon become quite intolerable did she not contrive, out of the goodness of her heart, to retain a keen and kindly interest in everything that concerns the welfare of her subjects. That her Majesty does feel this interest, and that it grows rather than diminishes as the years go by, every one knows who has been present on any of the innumerable occasions when the promoters of some charity or the directors of some educational institution have presented, with merciless precision, all the petty details of their projects or organizations for the examination of the imperial lady. The latest evidence of her

Majesty's benevolence is, however, more than usually striking. Since the founding of the Tōkyō Charity Hospital, where so many poor women and children are treated, the Empress has watched the institution closely, has bestowed on it patronage of the most active and helpful character, and has contributed handsomely to its funds. Little by little the hospital grew, extending its sphere of action and enlarging its ministrations, until the need of more capacious premises — a need familiar to such undertakings — began to be strongly felt. The Empress, knowing this, cast about for some means of assisting this project. To practice strict economy in her own personal expenses, and to devote whatever money might thus be saved from her yearly income to the aid of the hospital, appears to have suggested itself to her Majesty as the most feasible method of procedure. The result is, that a sum of 8,446 yen, 90 sen, and 8 rin has just been handed over to Dr. Takagi, the chief promoter and mainstay of the hospital, by Viscount Kagawa, one of her Majesty's chamberlains. There is something picturesque about these sen and rin. They represent an account minutely and faithfully kept between her Majesty's unavoidable expenses and the benevolent impulse that constantly urged her to curtail them. Such gracious acts of sterling effort command admiration and love."

Not very long ago, on one of her visits to the hospital, the Empress visited the children's ward, and took with her toys, which she gave with her own hand to each child there. When we consider that this hospital is free to the poorest and lowest person in Tōkyō, and that twenty years ago the persons of the Emperor and Empress were so sacred in the eyes of the people that no one but the highest nobles and the near officials of the court could come into their presence, — that even these high nobles were received at court by the Emperor at a distance of many feet, and his face even then could not be seen, — when we think of all this, we can begin to appreciate what the Empress Haru Ko has done in bridging the distance between herself and her people so that the poorest child of a beggar may receive a gift from her hand. In the country places to this day, there are peasants who yet believe that no one can look on the sacred face of the Emperor and live.

The school for the daughters of the nobles, to which I have before referred, is an institution whose welfare the Empress has very closely at heart, for she sees the need of rightly combining the new and the old in the education of the young girls who will so soon be filling places in the court. At the opening of the school the Empress was present, and herself made a speech to the scholars; and her visits, at intervals of one or two months, show her continued interest in the work that she has begun. Upon all state occasions, the scholars, standing with bowed heads as if in prayer, sing a little song written for them by the Empress herself; and at the graduating exercises, the speeches and addresses are listened to by her with the profoundest interest. The best specimens of poetry, painting, and composition done by the scholars are sent to the palace for her inspection, and some of these are kept by her in her own private rooms. When she visits the class-rooms, she does not simply pass in and pass out again, as if doing a formal duty, but sits for half an hour or so listening intently, and watching the faces of the scholars as they recite. In sewing and cooking classes (for the daughters of the nobles are taught to sew and cook), she sometimes speaks to the scholars, asking them questions. Upon one occasion she observed a young princess, a new-comer in the school, working somewhat awkwardly with needle and thimble. "The first time, Princess, is it not?" said the Empress, smiling, and the embarrassed Princess was obliged to confess that this was her first experience with those domestic implements.

Sometimes in her leisure hours — and they are rare in her busy life — the Empress amuses herself by receiving the little daughters of some imperial prince or nobleman, or even the children of some of the high officials. In the kindness of her heart, she takes great pleasure in seeing and talking to these little ones, some of whom are intensely awed by being in the presence of the Empress, while others, in their innocence, ignorant of all etiquette, prattle away unrestrainedly, to the great entertainment of the court ladies as well as of the Empress herself. These visits always end with some choice toy or gift, which the child takes home and keeps among her most valued treasures in remembrance of her imperial hostess. In this way the Empress relieves the loneliness of the great palace, where the sound of childish voices is seldom heard, for the Emperor's children are brought up in separate establishments, and only pay occasional visits to the palace, until they have passed early childhood.[1]

The present life of the Empress is not very different from that of European royalty. Her carriage and escort are frequently met with in the streets of Tōkyō as she goes or returns on one of her numerous visits of ceremony or beneficence. Policemen keep back the crowds of people who always gather to see the imperial carriage, and stand respectfully, but without demonstration, while the horsemen carrying the imperial insignia, followed

---

[1] The Emperor's children are placed, from birth, in the care of some noble or high official, who becomes the guardian of the child. Certain persons are appointed as attendants, and the child with its retinue lives in the establishment of the guardian, who is supposed to exercise his judgment and experience in the physical and mental training of the child.

closely by the carriages of the Empress and her attendants, pass by. The official Gazette announces almost daily visits by the Emperor, Empress, or other members of the imperial family, to different places of interest, — sometimes to various palaces in different parts of Tōkyō, at other times to schools, charitable institutions or exhibitions, as well as occasional visits to the homes of high officials or nobles, for which great preparations are made by those who have the honor of entertaining their Majesties.

Among the amusements within the palace grounds, one lately introduced, and at present in high favor, is that of horseback-riding, an exercise hitherto unknown to the ladies of Japan. The Empress and her ladies are said to be very fond of this active exercise, — an amusement forming a striking contrast to the quiet of former years.

The grounds about the palaces in Tōkyō are most beautifully laid out and cultivated, but not in that artificial manner, with regular flower beds and trees at certain equal distances, which is seen so often in the highly cultivated grounds of the rich in this country. The landscape gardening of Japan keeps unchanged the wildness and beauty of nature, and imitates it closely. The famous flowers, however, are, in the imperial gardens, changed by art and cultivated to their highest perfection, blooming each season for the enjoyment of the members of the court. Especially is attention given to the cultivation of the imperial flower of Japan, the chrysanthemum; and some day in November, when this flower is in its perfection, the gates of the Akasaka palace are thrown open to invited guests, who are received in person by the Emperor and Empress. Here the rarest species of this favorite flower, and the oddest colors and shapes, the results of much care and cultivation, are exhibited in spacious beds, shaded by temporary roofs of bamboo twigs and decorated with the imperial flags. This is the great chrysanthemum party of the Emperor, and another of similar character is given in the spring under the flower-laden boughs of the cherry trees.

In these various ways the Empress shows herself to her people, — a gracious and lovely figure, though distant, as she needs must be, from common, every-day life. Only by glimpses do the people know her, but those glimpses reveal enough to excite the warmest admiration, the most tender love. Childless herself, destined to see a child not her own, although her husband's, heir to the throne, the Empress devotes her lonely and not too happy life to the actual, personal study of the wants of daughters of her people, and side by side with Jingu,[1] the majestic but shadowy Empress of the past, should be enshrined in the hearts of the women of Japan the memory of Haru Ko, the leader of her countrywomen into that freer and happier life that is opening to them.

[1] Jingu Kōgō, like many of the heroic, half mythical figures of other nations, has suffered somewhat under the assaults of the modern historical criticism. Many of the best Japanese historians deny that she conquered Corea; some go so far as to doubt whether she had right to the title of Empress; all are sure that much of romance has gathered about the figure of this brave woman; but to the mass of the Japanese to-day, she is still an actual historic reality, and she represents to them in feminine form the Spirit of Japan. Whether she conquered Corea or no, she remains the prominent female figure upon the border line where the old barbaric life merges into the newer civilization, just as the present Empress, Haru Ko, stands upon the border line between the Eastern and the Western modes of thought and life.

Each marks the beginning of a new era, — the first, of the era of civilization and morality founded upon the teachings of Buddha and Confucius; the second, of the civilization and morality that have sprung from the teachings of Christ. Buddhism and Confucianism were elevating and civilizing, but failed to place the women of Japan upon even as high a plane as they had occupied in the old barbaric times. To Christianity they must look for the security and happiness which it has never failed to give to the wives and mothers of all Christian nations.

CHAPTER VII.

LIFE IN CASTLE AND YASHIKI.[1]

THE seclusion of the Emperors and the gathering of the reins of government into the hands of Shōguns was a gradual process, beginning not long after the introduction of Chinese civilization, and continuing to grow until Iyéyasŭ, the founder of the Tokugawa dynasty, through his code of laws, took from the Emperor the last vestige of real power, and perfected the feudal system which maintained the sway

---

[1] *Yashiki*, or spread-out house, was the name given to the palace and grounds of a daimiō's city residence, and also to the barracks occupied by his retainers, both in city and country. In the city the barracks of the samurai were built as a hollow square, in the centre of which stood the palace and grounds of their lord, and this whole place was the daimiō's *yashiki*. In the castle towns the daimiō's palace and gardens stood within the castle inclosure, surrounded by a moat, while the *yashikis* of the samurai were placed without the moat. They in turn were separated from the business part of the village sometimes by a second or third moat. By life in castle and *yashiki* we mean the life of the daimiō, whether in city or country.

of his house for two hundred and fifty years of peace.

The Emperor's court, with its literary and æsthetic quiet, its simplicity of life and complexity of etiquette, was the centre of the culture and art of Japan, but never the centre of luxury. After the growth of the Tokugawa power had secured for that house and its retainers great hereditary possessions, the Emperor's court was a mere shadow in the presence of the magnificence in which the Tokugawas and the daimiōs chose to live. The wealth of the country was in the hands of those who held the real power, and the Emperor was dependent for his support upon his great vassal, who held the land, collected the taxes, made the laws, and gave to his master whatever seemed necessary for his maintenance in the simple style of the old days, keeping for himself and for his retainers enough to make Yedo, the Tokugawa capital, the centre of a luxury far surpassing anything ever seen at the Emperor's own court. While the *kugé*, the old imperial nobility, formerly the governors of the provinces under the Emperors, lived in respectable but often extreme poverty at Kyōto, the landed nobility, or daimiōs, brought, after many struggles, under the sway of the Tokugawas, built for themselves palaces and pleasure gardens in the moated city of Yedo. At Yedo with its castle, its gardens, its *yashikis*, and its fortifications, was established a new court, more luxurious, but less artistic and cultivated, than the old court of Kyōto. In the various provinces, too, at every castle town, a little court arose about the castle, and the daimiō became not only the feudal chief, but the patron of literature and art among his people, as the years went by filling his *kura* with choice works of art, in lacquer, bronze, silver, and pottery, to be brought out on special occasions. These nobles, under a law of Iyémitsŭ, the third of the Tokugawa line, were compelled to spend half of each year at the city of the Shōguns; and each had his *yashiki*, or large house and garden, in the city. At this house, his family must reside permanently, as hostages for the loyalty of their lord while away. The annual journeys to and from Yedo were events not only in the lives of the daimiōs and their trains of retainers, but in the lives of the country people who lived along the roads by which they must travel. The time and style of each journey for each daimiō were rigidly prescribed in the laws of Iyémitsŭ, as well as the behavior of the country people who might meet the procession moving towards Yedo, or returning therefrom. When some noble, or any member of his family, was to pass through a certain section of the country, great preparations were made beforehand. Not only was traffic stopped along the route, but every door and window had to be closed. By no means was any one to show himself, or to look in any way upon the passing procession. To do so was to commit a profane deed, punishable by a fine. Among other things, no cooking was allowed on that day. All the food must be prepared the day before, as the air was supposed to become polluted by the smoke from the fires. Thus through crowded cities, full and busy with life, the daimiō in his curtained palanquin, with numerous retinue, would pass by; but wherever he approached, the place would be as deserted and silent as if plague-stricken. It is hardly necessary to add that these journeys, attended with so much ceremony and inconvenience to the people, were not as frequent as the trips now taken, at a moment's notice, from one city to another, by these very same men.

One story current in Tōkyō shows the narrowing effect of such seclusion. A noble who had traveled into Yedo, across one of the large bridges built over the Sumida River, remarked one day to his companions that he was greatly disappointed on seeing that bridge. "From the pictures," he said, "which I have seen, the bridge seemed alive with people, the centre of life and activity, but the artists must exaggerate, for not a soul was on the bridge when I passed by."

The castle of the Shōgun in Yedo, with its moats and fortifications, and its fine house and great *kura*, was reproduced on a small scale in the castles scattered through the country; and as in Yedo the *yashikis* of the daimios stood next to the inner moat of the castle, that the retainers might be ready to defend their lord at his earliest call, so in the provinces the *yashikis* of the samurai occupied a similar position about the daimiō's castle.

It is curious to see that, as the Shōgun

took away the military and temporal power of the Emperor, making of him only a figure-head without real power, so, to a certain degree, the daimiō gave up, little by little, the personal control of his own province, the power falling into the hands of ambitious samurai, who became the councilors of their lord. The samurai were the learned class and the military class; they were and are the life of Japan; and it is no wonder that the nobles, protected and shielded from the world, and growing up without much education, should have changed in the course of centuries from strong, brave warriors into the delicate, effeminate, luxury-loving nobles of the present day. Upon the loyalty and wisdom of the samurai, often upon some one man of undoubted ability, rested the greatness of the province and the prosperity of the master's house.

The life of the ladies in these daimiōs' houses is still a living memory to many of the older women of Japan; but it is a memory only, and has given place to a different state of things. The Emperor occupies the castle of the Shōgun to-day, and every daimiō's castle throughout the country is in the hands of the imperial government. The old pleasure gardens of the nobles are turned into arsenals, schools, public parks, and other improvements of the new era. But here and there one finds some conservative family of nobles still keeping up in some measure the customs of former times; and daimios' houses there are still in Tōkyō, though stripped of power and of retainers, where life goes on in many ways much as it did in the old days. In such a house as this, one finds ladies-in-waiting, of the samurai rank, who serve her ladyship — the daimiō's wife — in all personal service. In the old days, the daughters of the samurai were eager for the training in etiquette, and in all that belongs to nice housekeeping, that might be obtained by a few years of apprenticeship in a daimiō's house, and gladly assumed the most menial positions for the sake of the education and reputation to be gained by such training.

The wife and daughters of a daimiō led the quietest of lives, rarely passing beyond the four great walls that inclose the palace with its grounds. They saw the changes of the seasons in the flowers that bloomed in their lovely gardens, when, followed by numerous attendants, they slowly walked through the bamboo groves or under the bloom-laden boughs of the plum or cherry trees, forming their views of life, its pleasures, its responsibilities, and its meaning, within the narrow limits of the daimiō's *yashiki*.

Their mornings were passed in the adorning of their own persons, and in the elaborate dressing of their luxuriant hair; the afternoons were spent in the tea ceremony, in writing poetry, or the execution of a sort of silk mosaic that is a favorite variety of fancy work still among the ladies of Japan.

A story is told of one of the Tokugawa princesses that illustrates the amusements of the Shōgun's daughters, and the pains that were taken to gratify their wishes, however unreasonable. The cherry-trees of the castle gardens of Tōkyō are noted for their beauty when in bloom during the month of April. It is said that once a daughter of the Tokugawa house expressed a wish to give a garden party amid the blossoming cherry-trees in the month of December, and nothing would do but that her wishes must be carried out. Her retainers accordingly summoned to their aid skillful artificers, who from pink and white tissue paper produced myriads of cherry blossoms, so natural that they could hardly be distinguished from the real ones. These they fastened upon the trees in just such places as the real flowers would have chosen to occupy, and the happy princess gave her garden party in December under the pink mist of cherry blooms.

The children of a daimiō's wife occupied her attention but little. They were placed in the charge of careful attendants, and the mother, though allowed to see them when she wished, was deprived of the pleasure of constant intercourse with them, and had none of the mother's cares which form so large a part of life to an ordinary Japanese woman.

When we know that the average Japanese girl is brought up strictly by her own mother, and thoroughly drilled in obedience and in all that is proper as regards etiquette and the duties of woman, we can imagine the narrowness of the education of the daimiō's poor little daughter, surrounded, from early childhood, with numerous attendants of the strictest sort, to teach her all that is proper according to the highest and severest standards. Sometimes, by the whim or the indulgence of parents, or through exceptional circumstances in her surroundings, a samurai's daughter became more independent, more self-reliant, or better educated, than others of her rank; but such opportunities never came to the more carefully reared noble's daughter.

From her earliest childhood, she was addressed in the politest and most formal way, so that she could not help acquiring polite manners and speech. She was taught etiquette above all things, so that no rude action or speech would disgrace her rank; and that she should give due reverence to her superiors, courtesy to equals, and polite condescension to inferiors. She was taught especially to show kindness to the families under the rule of her father, and was early told of the noble's duty to protect and love his retainers, as a father loves and protects his children. From childhood, presents were made in her name to those around her, often without her previous knowledge or permission, and from them she would receive profuse thanks, — lessons in the delights of beneficence which could not fail to make their impression on the child princess. Even to inferiors she used the polite language,[1] and never the rude, brusque speech of men, or the careless phrases and expressions of the lower classes.

The education of the daimiō's daughter was conducted entirely at home.[2] Instead of going out to masters for instruction, she was taught by some one in the household, — one of her father's retainers, or perhaps a member of her own private retinue. Teachers for certain branches came from outside, and these were not expected to give the lesson within a certain time and hurry away, but they would remain,

---

[1] The Japanese language is full of expressions showing different shades of meaning in the politeness or respect implied. There are words and expressions which superiors in rank use to inferiors, or *vice versa*, and others used among equals. Some phrases belong especially to the language of the high-born, just as there are common expressions of the people. Some verbs in this extremely complex language must be altered in their termination according to the degree of honor in which the subject of the action is held in the speaker's mind.

[2] The establishment of the peeress' school, mentioned in the last chapter, is a great innovation upon the old-time ways of many of the aristocratic families.

conversing, sipping tea, and partaking of sweetmeats, until their noble pupil was ready to receive them. Hospitality required that the teacher be offered a meal after the lesson, and this meal etiquette would not permit him to refuse, so that both teacher and pupil must spend much time waiting for each other and for the lesson.

Pursued in this leisurely way, the education of the noble's daughter could not advance very rapidly, and it usually ended with an extremely early marriage; and the girl wife would sometimes play with her doll in the new home until the living baby took its place to the young mother.

The samurai women, who in one position or another were close attendants on these noble ladies, performing for them every act of service, were often women of more than average intelligence and education. From childhood to old age, the noble ladies were never without one or more of these maids of honor, close at hand to help or advise. Some entered the service in the lower positions for only a short period, leaving sooner or later to be married; for continued service in a daimiō's household meant a single life. Many of them remained in the palace all their days, leading lives of devotion to their mistress; the comfort and ease of which hardly compensated for the endless formalities and the monotonous seclusion.

Even the less responsible and more menial positions were not looked down upon, and the higher offices in the household were exceedingly honorable. When, once in a long while, a day's leave of absence was granted to one of these gentlewomen, and, loaded with presents sent by the daimiō's lady, she went on her visit to her home, she was received as a greatly honored member of her own family. The respect which was paid to her knowledge of etiquette and dress was never lessened because of the menial services she might have performed for those of noble blood.

The lady who was the head attendant, and those in the higher positions, had a great deal of power and influence in matters that concerned their mistress and the household; just as the male retainers decided for the prince, and in their own way, many of the affairs of the province. The few conservative old ladies, the last relics of the numerous retainers that once filled the castle, who still remain faithful in attendance in the homes now deprived of the grandeur of the olden times, look with horror upon the innovations of the present day, and sigh for the glory of old Japan. It is only upon compulsion that they give up many of the now useless formalities, and resign themselves to seeing their once so honored lords jostle elbow to elbow with the common citizen.

I shall never forget the horror of one old lady, attendant on a noble's daughter of high rank, just entering the peeress' school, when it was told her that each student must carry in her own bundle of books and arrange them herself, and that the attendants were not allowed in the class-room. The poor old lady was doubtless indignant at the thought that her noble-born mistress should have to perform even so slight a task as the arranging of her own desk unaided.

In the daimiōs' houses there was little of the culture or wit that graced the more aristocratic seclusion of Kyōto, and none of the duties and responsibilities that belonged to the samurai women, so that the life of the daimiō's lady was perhaps more purposeless, and less stimulating to the noble qualities, than the lives of any other of the women of Japan. Surrounded by endless restrictions of etiquette, lacking both the stimulus that comes from physical toil and that to be derived from intellectual exertion, the ladies of this class of the nobility simply vegetated. There is little wonder that the nobles degenerated both mentally and physically during the years when the Tokugawas held sway; for there was absolutely nothing in the lives of the women to fit them to be the wives and mothers of strong men. Delicate, dainty, refined, dexterous in all manner of little things but helpless to act for themselves, — ladies to the inmost core of their beings, with instincts of honor and of *noblesse oblige* appearing in them from earliest childhood, — the years of seclusion, of deference from hundreds of retainers, of constant instruction in the duties as well as the dignities of their position, have produced an abiding effect upon the minds of the women of this aristocracy, and to-day even the youngest and smallest of them have the virtues as well as the failings produced by nearly three centuries of training. They are lacking in force, in ambition, in clearness of thought, among a nation abounding in those qualities; but the national characteristics of dignity, charming manners, a quick sense of honor, and indomitable pride of race and nation, combined with a personal modesty almost deprecating in its humility, — these are found among the daughters of the nobles developed to their highest extent. With the qualities of gentleness and delicacy possessed by these ladies, which make them shrink from rough contact with the outer world, there are mingled the stronger qualities of bravery and physical courage. A daimiō's wife, as befitted the wife of a warrior and the daughter of long generations of brave men, never shrank from facing danger and death when necessary; and considered the taking of her own life an honorable and easy escape from being captured by her enemy.

Two or three little ripples from the past broke into my life in Tōkyō, giving a little insight into those old feudal times, and the customs that were common then, but that are now gone forever. A story was told me in Japan by a lady who had herself, as a child, witnessed the events narrated. It illustrates the responsibility felt by the retainers for their lord and his house. A daimiō fell into disgrace with the Shōgun, and was banished to his own capital, — a castle town several days' journey from Yedo, — as a punishment for some offense. The castle gates were closed, and no communication with the outer world allowed. During this period of disgrace, it happened that the noble fell ill, and died quite suddenly before his punishment was ended. His death under such circumstances was the most terrible thing that could befall either himself or his family, as his funeral must be without the ordinary tokens of respect; and his tombstone, instead of bearing tribute to his virtues, and the favor in which he had been held by his lord, must be simply the monument of his disgrace. This being the case, the retainers felt that these evils must be averted at any cost. Knowing that the Shōgun's anger was probably not so great as to make him wish to bring eternal disgrace to their dead lord, they at once decided to send a messenger to the Shōgun, begging for pardon on the plea of desperate illness, and asking the restoration of his favor before the approach of death. The death was not announced, but the floor of the room in which the man had died was lifted up, and the body let down to the ground beneath; and through all the town it was announced that the daimiō was hopelessly ill. Forty days passed before the Shōgun sent to the retainers the token that the disgrace was removed, and during all those forty days, in castle and barrack and village, the fiction of the daimiō's illness was kept up. As soon as the messengers returned, the body was drawn up again through the floor and placed on the bed; and all the retainers, from the least unto the greatest, were summoned into the room to congratulate their master upon his restoration to favor. One by one they entered the darkened room, prostrated themselves before the corpse, and uttered the formal words of congratulation. Then when all, even to the little girl who, grown to womanhood, told me the story, had been through the horrible ceremony, it was announced that the master was dead, — that he had died immediately after the return of the messenger with the good tidings of pardon.

All obstacles being thus removed, the funeral was celebrated with due pomp and circumstance; and the tombstone of the daimiō to-day gives no hint of the disgrace from which he so narrowly escaped.

Another instance very similar, throwing some light on the custom of adoption or *yoshii*, referred to in a previous chapter, was the case of a nobleman who died without children, and without an heir appointed to inherit his title. It would never have done, in sending in the official notice of death, to be unable to name the legal head of the house and the successor to the title. There was also no male relative to perform the office of chief mourner at the funeral; and so the death of the nobleman was kept secret, and his house showed no signs of mourning during a long period, until a son satisfactory to all the members of the household had been adopted. When the legal notice of the adoption had been sent in, and the son received into the family as heir, then, and only then, was the death of the lord announced, the period of mourning begun, and the funeral ceremony performed.

Upon one occasion I was visiting a Japanese lady, who knew the interest that I took in seeing and procuring the old-fashioned embroidered *kimonos*, which are now entirely out of style in Japan, and which can only be obtained at second-hand clothing stores, or at private sale. My friend said that she had just been shown an assortment of old garments which were offered at private sale by the heirs of a lady, recently deceased, who had once been a maid of honor in a daimiō's house. The clothes were still in the house, and were brought in, in a great basket, for my inspection. Very beautiful garments they were, of silk, crêpe, and linen, embroidered elaborately, and in extremely good order. Many of them seemed not to have been worn at all, but had been kept folded away for years, and only brought out when a fitting occasion came round at the proper season of the year. As we turned over the beautiful fabrics, a black broadcloth garment at the bottom of the basket aroused my curiosity, and I pulled it out and held it up for closer inspection. A curious garment it was, bound with white, and with a great white crest *appliqué* on the middle of the back. Curious white stripes gave the coat a military look, and it seemed appropriate rather to the wardrobe of some two-sworded warrior than to that of a gentlewoman of the old type. To the question, How did such a coat come to be in such a place? the older lady of the company — one to whom the old days were still the natural order and the new customs an exotic growth — explained that the garment rightfully belonged in the wardrobe of any lady-in-waiting in a daimiō's house, for it was made to wear in case of fire or attack when the men were away, and the women were expected to guard the premises. Further search among the relics of the past brought to light the rest of the costume: silk *hakama*, or full kilted trousers; a stiff, manlike black silk cap bound with a white band; and a spear cover of broadcloth, with a great white crest upon it, like the one on the broadcloth coat. These made up the uniform which must be donned in time of need by the ladies of the palace or the castle, for the defense of their lord's property. They had been folded away for twenty years among the embroidered robes, to come to light at last for the purpose of showing to a foreigner a phase of the old life that was so much a matter of course to the older Japanese that it never occurred to them even to mention it to a stranger. The elder lady of the house was wonderfully amused at my interest in these mute memorials of the past, and could never comprehend why I was willing to expend the sum of one dollar for the sake of gaining possession of a set of garments for which I could have no possible use. The uniform had probably never been worn in actual warfare, but its owner had been trained in the use of the long-handled spear, the cover of which she had kept stored away all these years; and had regarded herself as liable to be called into action at any time as one of the home guard, when the male retainers of her lord were in the field.

There are in the shops of Tōkyō to-day hundreds of colored prints illustrating the splendor of the Shōgunate; for the fine clothes, the pageants, the show and display that ended with the fall of the house of Tokugawa, are still dear to the popular mind. In these one sees reproduced, in more than their original brilliancy of coloring, the daimiōs, with their trains of uniformed retainers, proceeding in stately pageant to the palace of the Shōgun; the games, the dances, the reviews held before the Shōgun himself; the princess, with her train of ladies and attendants, visiting the cherry blossoms at Uyéno, or crossing some swift but shallow river on her journey to Yedo. There one sees the fleet of red-lacquered pleasure barges in which the Shōgun with his court sailed up the river to Mukōjima, in the spring, to view the cherry-trees which bloom along the banks for miles. One sees, too, the interiors of the daimiōs' houses, the intimate domestic scenes into which no outsider could ever penetrate. One picture shows the excitements consequent upon the advent of an heir to a noble house, — the happy mother on her couch, surrounded by brightly dressed ladies-in-waiting; the baby in the room adjoining; another group of brilliant beings preparing his bath; while down the long piazza, which opens upon the little courtyard in the centre of the house, one sees still other groups of servants, bringing the gifts with which the great mansion is flooded at such a time. Still further away, across the courtyard, are the doctors, holding learned consultation around a little table, and mixing medicines to secure the health and strength of both mother and baby.

The fall of the Shōgunate, and the abolition of castle and *yashiki*, have made a radical change in the fashions of dress in Japan. One sees no longer the beautiful embroidered robes, except upon the stage, for the abolition of the great leisure class has put the flowered *kimono* out of fashion. There are no courts, small and great, scattered all through the country, where the ladies must be dressed in changing styles for the changing seasons, and where the embroideries that imitate most closely the natural flowers are sure of a market. When one asks, as every foreigner is likely to ask, the Japanese ladies of one's acquaintance, "Why have you given up the beautiful embroideries and gorgeous colors that you used to wear?" the answer always is, "There are no daimiōs' houses now." And this is regarded as a sufficient explanation of the change.

I have in my possession to-day two dainty bits of the silk mosaic work before mentioned, the work of the sixteen-year-old wife of one of the proudest and most conservative of the present generation of nobles. A dainty little creature she was, with a face upon which her two years of wifehood and one year of motherhood had left no trace of care. Living amid her host of ladies and women servants, most of them older and wiser than herself; having no care and no amusements save the easy task of keeping herself pretty and well-dressed, and the amusement of watching her baby grow, and hearing the chance rumors that might come to her from the great new world into which her husband daily went, but with which she herself never mingled, — her days were one pleasant, monotonous round, unawakening alike either to soul or intellect. Into this life of remoteness from all that belongs to the new era, imagine the excitement produced by the advent of a foreign lady, with an educated dog, whose wonderful intelligence had been already related to her by one of her own ladies-in-waiting. I shall always believe that my invitation into that exclusive house was due largely to the reports of my dog, carried to its proprietors by one of the lady servitors who had seen him perform upon one occasion. Certain it is that the first words of the little lady of the house to me were a question about the dog; and her last act of politeness to our party was a warm embrace of the handsome collie, who had given unimpeachable evidence that he understood a great deal of English, — a tongue which the daimiō himself was painfully learning. The dainty child-wife with both arms buried in the heavy ruff of the astonished dog is a picture that comes to me often, and that brings up most pathetically the monotony of an existence into which so small a thing can bring so much. The lifelike black and white silk puppy, the creeping baby doll from Kyōto, the silk mosaic box and chopstick case, — the work of my lady's delicate fingers, — are most agreeable reminders of the kindness and sweetness of the little wife, whose sixteen summers have been spent among the surroundings of thirty years ago, and who lives, like the enchanted princess of the fairy tales, wrapped about by a spell which separates her from the bustling world of to-day. The product of the past, — the daughter of the last of the Shōguns, — she dwells in her enchanted house, among the relics of a past which is still the present to her and to her household. So lovely, so æsthetic, so dainty and charming seems the world into which one enters there, that one would not care to break the spell that holds it as it is, and let the girl-wife, with her gentlewomen and her kneeling servants, hurry forward into the busy, perplexing life of to-day. May time deal gently with her and hers, nor rudely break the enchantment that surrounds her!

CHAPTER VIII.

SAMURAI WOMEN.

Samurai was the name given to the military class among the Japanese, — a class intermediate between the Emperor and his nobles and the great mass of the common people who were engaged in agriculture, mechanical arts, or trade. Upon the samurai rested the defense of the country from enemies at home or abroad, as well as the preservation of literature and learning, and the conduct of all official business. At the time of the fall of feudalism, there were, among the thirty-four millions of Japanese, about two million samurai; and in this class, in the broadest sense of the word, must be included the daimiōs, as well as their two-sworded retainers. But as the greater among the samurai were distinguished by special class names, the word as commonly used, and as used throughout this work, applies to the military class, who served the Shōgun and the daimiōs, and who were supported by yearly allowances from the treasuries of their lords. These form a distinct class, actuated by motives quite different from those of the lower classes, and filling a great place in the history of the country. As the nobility, through long inheritance of power and wealth, became weak in body and mind, the samurai grew to be, more and more, not only the sword, but the brain of Japan; and to-day the great work of bringing the country out of the middle ages into the nineteenth century is being performed by the samurai more than by any other class.

What, it may be asked, are the traits of the samurai which distinguish them, and make them such honored types of the perfect Japanese gentleman, so that to live and die worthy the name of samurai was the highest ambition of the soldier? The samurai's duty may be expressed in one word, loyalty,—loyalty to his lord and master, and loyalty to his country,—loyalty so true and deep that for it all human ties, hopes, and affections, wife, children, and home, must be sacrificed if necessary. Those who have read the tale of "The Loyal Rōnins"[1] — a story which has been so well told by Mitford, Dickens, and Greey that many readers must be already familiar with it — will remember that the head councilor and retainer, Oishi, in his deep desire for revenge for his lord's unjust death, divorces his wife and sends off his children, that they may not distract his thoughts from his plans; and performs his famous act of revenge without once seeing his wife, only letting her know at his death his faithfulness to her and the true cause of his seeming cruelty. And the wife, far from feeling wronged by such an act, only glories in the loyalty of her husband, who threw aside everything to fulfill his one great duty, even though she herself was his unhappy victim.

The true samurai is always brave, never fearing death or suffering in any form. Life and death are alike to him, if no disgrace is attached to his name.

An incident comes into my mind which

[1] *Rōnin* was the term applied to a samurai who had lost his master, and owed no feudal allegiance to any daimiō. The exact meaning of the word is *wave-man*, signifying one who wanders to and fro without purpose, like a wave driven by the wind.

may serve as an example of the samurai spirit, — a spirit which has filled the history of Japan with heroic deeds. It is the story of a long siege, at the end of which the little garrison in the besieged castle was reduced to the last stages of endurance, though hourly expecting reinforcement. In this state of affairs, the great question is, whether to wait for the expected aid, or to surrender immediately, and the answer to the question can only be obtained through a knowledge of the enemy's strength. At this juncture, one of the samurai volunteers to steal into the camp of the besiegers, inspect their forces, and report their strength before the final decision is made. He disguises himself, and through various chances is able to penetrate, unsuspected, into the midst of the enemy's camp. He discovers that the besiegers are so weak that they cannot maintain the siege much longer, but while returning to the castle he is recognized and taken by the enemy. His captors give him one chance for escape from the horrible death of crucifixion. He is to go to the edge of the moat, and, standing on an elevated place, shout out to the soldiers that they must surrender, for the forces are too strong for them. He seemingly consents to this, and, led down to the water's edge, he sees across the moat his wife and child, who greet him with demonstrations of joy. To her he waves his hand; then, bravely and loudly, so that it may be heard by friend and foe, he shouts out the true tidings, "Wait for reinforcement at any cost, for the besiegers are weak and will soon have to give up." At these words his enraged enemies seize him and put him to a death of horrible torture, but he smiles in their faces as he tells them the sweetness of such a sacrifice for his master. Japanese history abounds with heroic deeds of blood displaying the indomitable courage of the samurai. In the reading of them, we are often reminded of the Spartan spirit of warfare, and samurai women are in some ways very like those Spartan mothers who would rather die than see their sons branded as cowards.

The implicit obedience which samurai gave their lords, when conflicting with feelings of loyalty to their country, often produced two opposing forces which had to be overcome. When the daimiō gave orders that the keener-sighted retainer felt would not be for the good of the house, he had either to disobey his lord, or act against his feeling of loyalty. Divided between the two duties, the samurai would usually do as he thought right for his country or his lord, disobeying his master's orders; write a confession of his real motives; and save his name from disgrace by committing suicide. By this act he would atone for his disobedience, and his loyalty would never be questioned.

The now abolished custom of *hara-kiri*, or the voluntary taking of one's life to avoid disgrace, and blot out entirely or partially the stain on an honorable name, is a curious custom which has come down from old times. The ancient heroes stabbed themselves as calmly as they did their enemies, and women as well as men knew how to use the short sword [1] worn always

[1] The samurai always wore two swords, a long one for fighting only, and a short one for defense when possible, but, as a last resort, for *hara-kiri*. The sword is the emblem of the samurai spirit, and as such is respected and honored. A samurai took pride in keeping his swords as sharp and shining as was possible. He was never seen without the two swords, but the longer one he removed and left at the front door when he entered the house of a friend. To use a sword badly, to harm or injure it, or to step over it, was considered an insult to the owner.

at the side of the samurai, his last and easy escape from shameful death.

The young men of this class, as well as their masters, the daimiōs, were early instructed in the method of this self-stabbing, so that it might be cleanly and easily done, for a bloody and unseemly death would not redound to the honor of the suicide. The fatal cut was not instantaneous in its effect, and there was always opportunity for that display of courage — that show of disregard for death or pain — which was expected of the brave man.

The *hara-kiri* was of course a last resort, but it was an honorable death. The vulgar criminal must be put to death by the hands of others, but the nobler samurai, who never cares to survive disgrace, was condemned to *hara-kiri* if found guilty of actions worthy of death. Not to be allowed to do this, but to be executed in the common way, was a double disgrace to a samurai. Even to this day, when crimes such as the assassination of a minister of state are committed, in the mistaken belief that the act is for the good of the country, the idea on the part of the assassin is never to escape detection. He calmly gives himself up to justice or takes his own life,[1] stating his motive for the deed; and, believing himself justified in the act, is willing that his life should be the cost.

The old samurai was proud of his rank, his honorable vocation, his responsibility; proud of his ignorance of trade and barter and of his disregard for the sordid cares of the world, regarding as far beneath him all occupations but those of arms. Wealth, as artisan or farmer, rarely tempted him to sink into the lower ranks; and his support from the daimiō, often a mere pittance, insured to him more respect and greater privileges than wealth as a héimin. To this day even, this feeling exists. Preference for rank or position, rather than for mere salary, remains strongly among the present generation, so that official positions are more sought after than the more lucrative occupations of trade. Japan

[1] Kurushima, who attempted to take the life of Okuma, the late Minister of Foreign Affairs, as recently as 1889, committed suicide immediately after throwing the dynamite bomb which caused the minister the loss of his leg. This was the more remarkable in that, at the time of his death, the assassin supposed that his victim had escaped all injury.

is flooded with small officials, and yet the samurai now is obliged to lay down his sword and devote his time to the once despised trades, and to learn how important are the arts of peace compared with those of war.

The dislike of anything suggestive of trade or barter — of services and actions springing, not from duty and from the heart, but from the desire of gain — has strongly tinted many little customs of the day, often misunderstood and misconstrued by foreigners. In old Japan, experience and knowledge could not be bought and sold. Physicians did not charge for their services, but on the contrary would decline to name or even receive a compensation from those in their own clan. Patients, on their side, were too proud to accept services free, and would send to the physicians, not as pay exactly, but more as a gift or a token of gratitude, a sum of money which varied according to the means of the giver, as well as to the amount of service received. Daimiōs did not send to ask a teacher how much an hour his time was worth, and then arrange the lessons accordingly; the teacher was not insulted by being expected to barter his knowledge for so much filthy lucre, but was merely asked whether his time and convenience would allow of his taking extra teaching. The request was made, not as a matter of give and take, but a favor to be granted. Due compensation, however, would never fail to be made, — of this the teacher could be sure, — but no agreement was ever considered necessary.

With this feeling yet remaining in Japan, — this dislike of contracts, and exact charges for professional services, — we can imagine the inward disgust of the samurai at the business-like habits of the foreigners with whom he has to deal. On the other hand, his feelings are not appreciated by the foreigner, and his actions clash with the European and American ideas of independence and self-respect. In Japan a present of money is more honorable than pay, whereas in America pay is much more honorable than a present.

The samurai of to-day is rapidly imbibing new ideas, and is learning to see the world from a Western point of view; but his thoughts and actions are still moulded on the ideas of old Japan, and it will be a long time before the loyal, faithful, but proud spirit of the samurai will die out. The pride of clan is now changed to pride of race; loyalty to feudal chief has become loyalty to the Emperor as sovereign; and the old traits of character exist under the European costumes of to-day, as under the flowing robes of the two-sworded retainer.

It is this same spirit of loyalty that has made it hard for Christianity to get a foothold in Japan. The Emperor was the representative of the gods of Japan. To embrace a new religion seemed a desertion of him, and the following of the strange gods of the foreigner. The work of the Catholic missionaries which ended so disastrously in 1637 has left the impression that a Christian is bound to offer allegiance to the Pope in much the same way as the Emperor now receives it from his people; and the bitterness of such a thought has made many refuse to hear what Christianity really is. Such words as "King" and "Lord" they have understood as referring to temporal things, and it has taken years to undo this prejudice; a feeling in no way surprising when we consider how the Jesuit missionaries once interfered with political movements in Japan.

So bitter was this feeling, when Japan was first opened, that a native Christian was at once branded as a traitor to his country, and very severe was the persecution against all Christians. Missionaries at one time dared not acknowledge themselves as such, and lived in danger of their lives; and the Japanese Christian who remained faithful did so knowing that he was despised and hated. I know of one mother who, finding command and entreaty alike unavailing to move her son, a convert to the new religion, threatened to commit suicide, feeling that the disgrace which had fallen on the family could only be wiped out with her death. Happily, all this is of the past, and to-day the samurai has found that he can reconcile the new religion with his loyalty to Japan, and that in receiving the one he is not led to betray the other.

The women of the samurai have shared with the men the responsibilities of their rank, and the pride that comes from hereditary positions of responsibility. A woman's first duty in all ranks of society is obedience; but sacrifice of self, in however horrible a way, was a duty most cheerfully and willingly performed, when by such sacrifice father, husband, or son might be the better able to fulfill his duty towards his feudal superior. The women in the daimiōs' castles who were taught fencing, drilled and uniformed, and relied upon to defend the castle in case of need, were women of this class, — women whose husbands and fathers were soldiers, and in whose veins ran the blood of generations of fighting ancestors. Gentle, feminine, delicate as they were, there was a possibility of martial prowess about them when the need for it came; and the long education in obedience and loyalty did not fail to produce the desired results. Death, and ignominy worse than death, could be met bravely, but disgrace involving loss of honor to husband or feudal lord was the one thing that must be avoided at all hazards. It was my good fortune, many years ago, to make the acquaintance of a little Japanese girl who had lived in the midst of the siege of Wakamatsu, the city in which the Shōgun's forces made their last stand for their lord and the system that he represented. As the Emperor's forces marched upon the castle town, moat after moat was taken, until at last men, women, and children took refuge within the citadel itself to defend it until the last gasp. The bombs of the besiegers fell crashing into the castle precincts, killing the women as they worked at whatever they could do in aid of the defenders; and even the little girls ran back and forth, amid the rain of bullets and balls, carrying cartridges, which the women were making within the castle, to the men who were defending the walls. "Were n't you afraid?" we asked the delicate child, when she told us of her own share in the defense. "No," was the answer. A small but dangerous sword, of the finest Japanese steel, was shown us as the sword that she wore in her belt during all those days of war and tumult. "Why did you wear the sword?" we asked. "So that I would have it if I was taken prisoner." "What would you have done with it?" was the next question, for we could not believe that a child of eight would undertake to defend herself against armed soldiers with that little sword. "I would have killed myself," was the answer, with a flash of the eye that showed her quite capable of committing the act in case of need.

In the olden times, when the spirit of warfare was strong and justice but scantily administered, revenge for personal insult, or for the death of father or lord, fell upon the children, or the retainers. Sometimes the bloody deed has fallen to the lot of a woman, to some weak and feeble girl, who, in many a tale, has braved all the difficulties that beset a woman's path, devoted her life to an act of vengeance, and, with the courage of a man, has often successfully consummated her revenge.

One of the tales of old Japan, and a favorite subject of theatrical representation, is the death and revenge of a lady in a daimiō's palace. Onoyé, a daughter of the people, child of a merchant, has by chance risen to the position of lady-in-waiting to a daimiō's wife, — a thing so uncommon that it has roused the jealousy of the other ladies, who are of the samurai class. Iwafuji, one of the highest and proudest ladies at the court, takes pains on every occasion to insult and torment the poor, unoffending Onoyé, whom she cannot bear to have as an associate. She constantly reminds her of her inferior birth, and at last challenges her to a trial in fencing, in which accomplishment Onoyé is not proficient, having lacked the proper training in her early life. At last the hatred and anger of Iwáfuji culminate in a frenzy of rage; she forgets herself, and strikes the meek and gentle Onoyé with her sandal, — the worst insult that could be offered to any one.

Onoyé, overcome by this deep disgrace offered her in public, returns from the main palace to her own apartments, and ponders long and deeply, in the bitterness of her soul, how to wipe out the disgrace of an insult by such an enemy.

Her own faithful maid, seeing her disordered hair and anxious looks, perceives some secret trouble, which her mistress will not disclose, and tries, while performing her acts of service, to dispel the gloom by telling gayly all the gossip of the day. This maid, O Haru, is a type of the clever faithful servant. She is really of higher birth than her mistress, for, though she has been obliged to go out to service, she was born of a samurai family. Onoyé, while listening to the talk of her servant, has made up her mind that only one thing can blot out her disgrace, and that is to commit suicide. She hastily pens a farewell to her family, for the deed must not be delayed, and sends with the letter the token of her disgrace, — Iwafuji's sandal, which she has kept. O Haru is sent on this errand, and, unconscious of the ill-news she is bearing, she starts out. On the way, the ominous croak of the ravens, who are making a dismal noise, — a presage of ill-luck, — frightens the observant O Haru. A little further on, the strap of her clog breaks, — a still more alarming sign. Thoroughly frightened, O Haru turns back, and reaches her mistress' room in time to find that the fatal deed is done, and her mistress is dying. O Haru is heart-broken, learns the whole truth, and vows vengeance on the enemy of her loved mistress.

O Haru, unlike Onoyé, is thoroughly trained in fencing. An occasion arises when she returns to Iwafuji in public the malicious blow, and with the same sandal, which she has kept as a sign of her revenge. She then challenges Iwafuji, in behalf of the dead, to a trial in fencing. The haughty Iwafuji is forced to accept, and is thoroughly defeated and shamed before the spectators. The whole truth is now made known, and the daimiō, who admires and appreciates the spirit of O Haru, sends for her, and raises her from her low position to fill the post of her dead mistress.

These stories show the spirit of the samurai women; they can suffer death bravely, even joyfully, at their own hands or the hands of husband or father, to avoid or wipe out any disgrace which they regard as a loss of honor; but they will as bravely and patiently subject themselves to a life of shame and ignominy, worse than death, for the sake of gaining for husband or father the means of carrying out a feudal obligation. There is a pathetic scene, in one of the most famous of the Japanese historical dramas, in which one seems to get the moral perspective of the ideal Japanese woman, as one cannot get it in any other way. The play is founded on the story of "The Loyal Rōnins," referred to in the beginning of this chapter. The loyal rōnins are plotting to avenge the death of their master upon the daimiō whose cupidity and injustice have brought it about. As there is danger of disloyalty even in their own ranks, Oishi, the leader of the dead daimiō's retainers, displays great caution in the selection of his fellow-conspirators, and practices every artifice to secure absolute secrecy for his plans. One young man, who was in disgrace with his lord at the time of his death, applies to be admitted within the circle of conspirators; but as it is suspected that he may not be true to the cause, a payment in money is exacted from him as a pledge of his honorable intentions. It is thus made his first duty to redeem his honor from all suspicion by the payment of the money, in order that he may perform his feudal obligation of avenging the death of his lord. But the young man is poor; he has married a poor girl, and has agreed to support not only his wife, but her old parents as well, and the payment is impossible for him. In this emergency, his wife, at the suggestion of her parents, proposes, as the only way, to sell herself, for a term of two years, to the proprietor of a house of pleasure, that she may by this vile servitude enable her husband to escape the dishonor that must come to him if he fails to fulfill his feudal duty. Negotiations are entered into, the contract is made, and an advance payment is given which will furnish money enough for the pledge required by the conspirators. All this is done without the knowledge of the husband, lest his love for his wife and his grief for the sacrifice prevent him from accepting the only means left to prove his loyalty. The noble wife even plans to leave her home while he is away on a hunting expedition, and so spare him the pain of parting. His emotion upon learning of this venture in business is not of wrath at the disgrace that has overtaken his family, but simply of grief that his wife and her parents must make so great a sacrifice to save his honor. It is a terrible affliction, but it is not a disgrace in any way parallel to the disgrace of disloyalty to his lord. And the heroic wife, when the men come to carry her away, is upheld through all the trying farewells by the consciousness that she is making as noble a sacrifice of herself as did the wife of Yamato Daké when she leaped into the sea to avert the wrath of the sea-god from her husband. The Japanese, both men and women, knowing this story and many others similar in character, can see, as we cannot from our point of view, that, even if the body be defiled, there is no defilement of the soul, for the woman is fulfilling her highest duty in sacrificing all, even her dearest possession, for the honor of her husband. It is a climax of self-abnegation that brings nothing but honor to the soul of her who reaches it. Japanese women who read this story feel profound pity for the poor wife, and a horror of a sacrifice that binds her to a life which outwardly, to the Japanese mind even, is the lowest depth a woman ever reaches. But they do not despise her for the act; nor would they refuse to receive her even were she to appear in living form to-day in any Japanese home, where, thanks to happier fortunes, such sacrifices are not demanded. Just at this point is the difference of moral perspective that foreigners visiting Japan find so hard to understand, and that leads many, who have lived in the country the longest, to believe that there is no modesty and purity among Japanese women. It is this that makes it possible for the vilest of stories, and those that have the least foundation in fact, to find easy belief among foreigners, even if they be told about the purest, most high-minded, and most honorable of Japanese women. Our maidens, as they grow to womanhood, are taught that anything is better than personal dishonor, and their maidenly instincts side with the teaching. With us, a virtuous woman does not mean a brave, a heroic, an unselfish, or self-sacrificing woman, but means simply one who keeps herself from personal dishonor. Chastity is the supreme virtue for a woman; all other virtues are secondary compared with it. This is our point of view, and the whole perspective is arranged with that virtue in the foreground. Dismiss this for a moment, and consider the moral training of the Japanese maiden. From earliest youth until she reaches maturity, she is constantly taught that obedience and loyalty are the supreme virtues, which must be preserved even at the sacrifice of all other and lesser virtues. She is told that for the good of father or husband she must be willing to meet any danger, endure any dishonor, perpetrate any crime, give up any treasure. She must consider that nothing belonging solely to herself is of any importance compared with the good of her master, her family, or her country. Place this thought of obedience and loyalty, to the point of absolute self-abnegation, in the foreground, and your perspective is altered, the other virtues occupying places of varying importance. Because a Japanese woman will sometimes sacrifice her personal virtue for the sake of father or husband, does it follow that all Japanese women are unchaste and impure? In many cases this sacrifice is the noblest that she believes possible, and she goes to it, as she would go to death in any dreadful form, for those whom she loves, and to whom she owes the duty of obedience. The Japanese maiden grows to womanhood no less pure and modest than our own girls, but our girls are never called upon to sacrifice their modesty for the sake of those whom they love best; nor is it expected of any woman in this country that she exist solely for the good of some one else, in whatever way he chooses to use her, during all the years of her life. Let us take this difference into our thought in forming our judgment, and let us rather seek the causes that underlie the actions than pass judgment upon the actions themselves. From a close study of the characters of many Japanese women and girls, I am quite convinced that few women in any country do their duty, as they see it, more nobly, more single-mindedly, and more satisfactorily to those about them, than the women of Japan.

Many argue that the purity of Japanese women, as compared with the men, the ready obedience which they yield, their sweet characters and unselfish devotion as wives and mothers, are merely the results of the restraint under which they live, and that they are too weak to be allowed to enjoy freedom of thought and action. Whether this be true or no is a point which we leave for others to take up, as time shall have provided new data for reasoning on the subject.

To me, the sense of duty seems to be strongly developed in the Japanese women, especially in those of the samurai class. Conscience seems as active, though often in a different manner, as the old-fashioned New England conscience, transmitted through the bluest of Puritan blood. And when a duty has once been recognized as such, no timidity, or mortification, or fear of ridicule will prevent the performance of it. A case comes to my mind now of a young girl of sixteen, who made public confession before her schoolmates of shortcomings of which none of them knew, for the sake of easing her troubled conscience and warning her schoolmates against similar errors. The circumstances were as follows: The young girl had recently lost her grandmother, a most loving and affectionate old lady, who had taken the place of a mother to the child from her earliest infancy. In a somewhat unhappy home, the love of the old grandmother was the one bright spot; and when she was taken away, the poor, lonely child's memory recalled all of her own shortcomings to this beloved friend; and, too late to make amendment to the old lady herself, she dwelt on her own undutifulness, and decided that she must by some means do penance, or make atonement for her fault. She might, if she made a confession before her schoolmates, warn them against similar mistakes; and accordingly she prepared, for the literary society in which the girls took what part they chose, a long confession, written in poetical style, and read it before her schoolmates and teachers. It was a terrible ordeal, as one could see by the blushing face and breaking voice, often choked with sobs; and when at the conclusion she urged her friends to behave in such a way to their dear ones that they need never suffer what she had had to endure since her grandmother's death, there was not a dry eye in the room, and many of the girls were sobbing aloud. It was a curious expiation and a touching one, but one not in the least exceptional or uncharacteristic of the spirit of duty that actuates the best women of the samurai class.

Here is another instance which illustrates this sense of duty, and desire of atoning for past mistakes or sins. At the time of the overthrow of the feudal system, the samurai, bred to loyalty to their own feudal superiors as their highest duty, found themselves ranged on different sides in the struggle, according to the positions in which their lords placed themselves. At the end of the struggle, those who had followed their daimiōs to the field, in defense of the Shōgunate, found that they had been fighting against the Emperor, the

Son of Heaven himself, who had at last emerged from the seclusion of centuries to govern his own empire. Thus the supporters of the Shōgunate, while absolutely loyal to their daimiōs, had been disloyal to the higher power of the Emperor; and had put themselves in the position of traitors to their country. There was a conflict of principles there somewhat similar to that which took place in our Civil War, when, in the South, he who was true to his State became a traitor to his country, and he who was true to his country became a traitor to his State. Two ladies of the finest samurai type had, with absolute loyalty to a lost cause, aided by every means in their power in the defense of the city of Wakamatsu against the victorious forces of the Emperor. They had held on to the bitter end, and had been banished, with others of their family and clan, to a remote province, for some years after the end of the war. In 1877, eleven years after the close of the War of the Restoration, a rebellion broke out in the south which required a considerable expenditure of blood and money for its suppression. When the new war began, these two ladies presented a petition to the government, in which they begged that they might be allowed to make amends for their former position of opposition to the Emperor, by going with the army to the field as hospital nurses. At that time, no lady in Japan had ever gone to the front to nurse the wounded soldiers; but to those two brave women was granted the privilege of making atonement for past disloyalty, by the exercise of the skill and nerve that they had gained in their experience of war against the Emperor, in the nursing of soldiers wounded in his defense.

In the old days, the women of the samurai class fulfilled most nobly the duties that fell to their lot. As wives and mothers in time of peace, they performed their work faithfully in the quiet of their homes; and, their time filled with household cares, they busied themselves with the smaller duties of life. As the wives and mothers of soldiers, they cultivated the heroic spirit befitting their position, fearing no danger save such as involved disgrace. As the home-guard in time of need, they stood ready to defend their master's possessions with their own lives; as gentlewomen and ladies-in-waiting at the court of the daimio or the Shōgun, they cultivated the arts and accomplishments required for their position, and veiled the martial spirit that dwelt within them under an exterior as feminine, as gracious, as cultivated and charming, as that of any ladies of Europe or America. To-day in the new Japan, where the samurai have no longer their yearly allowance from their lords and their feudal duties, but, scattered through the whole nation, are engaged in all the arts and trades, and are infusing the old spirit into the new life, what are the women doing? As the government of the land to-day lies in the hands of the samurai men under the Emperor, so the progress of the women, the new ideas of work for women, are in the hands of the samurai women, led by the Empress. Wherever there is progress among the women, wherever they are looking about for new opportunities, entering new occupations, elevating the home, opening hospitals, industrial schools, asylums, there you will find the leading spirits always of the samurai class. In the recent changes, some of this class have risen above their former state and joined the ranks of the nobility; and there the presence of the samurai spirit infuses new life into the aristocracy. So, too, the changes that have raised some have lowered others, and the samurai is now to be found in the formerly despised occupations of trade and industry, among the merchants, the farmers, the fishermen, the artisans, and the domestic servants. But wherever his lot is cast, the old training, the old ideals, the old pride of family, still keep him separate from his present rank, and, instead of pulling him down to the level of those about him, tend to raise that level by the example of honor and intelligence that he sets. The changed fortunes were not met without a murmur. Most of the outrages, the reactionary movements, the riots and inflammatory speeches and writings, that characterized the long period of disquiet following the Restoration, came from men of this class, who saw their support taken from them, leaving them unable to dig and ashamed to beg. But the greater part of them went sturdily to work, in government positions if they could get them, in the army, on the police force, on the farm, in the shop, at trades, at service,

— even to the humble work of wheeling a *jinrikisha*, if other honest occupation could not be found; and the women shared patiently and bravely the changed fortunes of the men, doing whatever they could toward bettering them. The samurai women today are eagerly working into the positions of teachers, interpreters, trained nurses, and whatever other places there are which may be honorably occupied by women. The girls' schools, both government and private, find many of their pupils among the samurai class; and their deference and obedience to their teachers and superiors, their ambition and keen sense of honor in the school-room, show the influence of the samurai feeling over new Japan. To the samurai women belongs the task — and they have already begun to perform it — of establishing upon a broader and surer foundation the position of women in their own country. They, as the most intelligent, will be the first to perceive the remedy for present evils, and will, if I mistake not, move heaven and earth, at some time in the near future, to have that remedy applied to their own case. Most of them read the literature of the day, some of them in at least one language beside their own; a few have had the benefit of travel abroad, and have seen what the home and the family are in Christian lands. There is as much of the unconquerable spirit of the samurai to-day in the women as in the men; and it will not be very long before that spirit will begin to show itself in working for the establishment of their homes and families upon some stronger basis than the will of the husband and father.

CHAPTER IX.

PEASANT WOMEN.

THE great héimin class includes not only the peasants of Japan, but also the artisans and merchants; artisans ranking below farmers, and merchants below artisans, in the social structure. It includes the whole of the common people, except such as were in former times altogether below the level of respectability, the *éta* and *hinin*,[1] — outcasts who lived by begging, slaughtering animals, caring for dead bodies, tanning skins, and other employments which rendered them unclean according to the old notions. From very early times the agricultural class has been sharply divided from the samurai or mili-

---

[1] The laws against the *éta* and *hinin*, making of them a distinct, unclean class, and forbidding their intermarriage with any of the higher classes, have recently been abolished. There is now no rank distinction of any practical value, except that between noble and common people. Héimin and samurai are now indiscriminately mingled.

tary. Here and there one from the peasantry mounts by force of his personal qualities into the higher ranks, for there is no caste system that prevents the passing from one class into another, — only a class prejudice that serves very nearly the same purpose, in keeping samurai and héimin in their places, that the race prejudice in this country serves in confining the negroes, North and South, to certain positions and occupations. The first division of the military from the peasantry occurred in the eighth century, and since then the peculiar circumstances of each class have tended to produce quite different characteristics in persons originally of the same stock. To the soldier class have fallen learning, skill in arms and horsemanship, opportunities to rise to places of honor and power, lives free from sordid care in regard to the daily rice, and in which noble ideas of duty and loyalty can spring up and bear fruit in heroic deeds. To the peasant, tilling his little rice-field year after year, have come the heavy burdens of taxation; the grinding toil for a mere pittance of food for himself and his family; the patient bearing of all things imposed by his superiors, with little hope of gain for himself, whatever change the fortunes of war may bring to those above him in the social scale. Is there wonder that, as the years have gone by, his wits have grown heavy under his daily drudgery; that he knows little and understands less of the changes that are taking place in his native land; that he is easily moved by only one thing, and that the failure of his crops, or the shortening of his returns from his land by heavier taxation? This is true of the héimin as a class: they are conservative, fearing that change will but tend to make harder a lot that is none too easy; and though peaceable and gentle usually, they may be moved to blind acts of riot and bloodshed by any political change that seems likely to produce heavier taxation, or even by a failure of their crops, when they see themselves and their families starving while the military and official classes have enough and to spare. But though, as a class, the farmers are ignorant and heavy, they are seldom entirely illiterate; and everywhere, throughout the country, one finds men belonging to this class who are well educated and have risen to positions of much responsibility and power, and are able to hold their own, and think for themselves and for their brethren. From an article in the "Tōkyō Mail," entitled "A Memorialist of the Latter Days of the Tokugawa Government," I quote passages which show the thoughts of one of the héimin upon the condition of his own class about the year 1850. It is from a petition sent to the Shōgun by the head-man of the village of Ogushi.

The first point in the petition is, that there is a growing tendency to luxury among the military and official classes. "It is useless to issue orders commanding peasants and others to be frugal and industrious, when those in power, whose duty it is to show a good example to the people, are themselves steeped in luxury and idleness." He ventures to reproach the Shōguns themselves by pointing to the extravagance with which they have decorated the mausoleums at Nikkō and elsewhere. "Is this," he asks, "in keeping with the intentions of the glorious founder of your dynasty? Look at the shrines in Isé and elsewhere, and at the sepulchres of the Emperors of successive ages. Is gold or silver used in decorating them?" He then turns to the vassals of the Shōgun, and charges them with being tyrannical, rapacious, and low-minded. "Samurai," he continues,—"samurai are finely attired, but how contemptible they look in the eyes of those peasants who know how to be contented with what they have!"

Further on in the same memorial, he points out what he regards as a grave mistake in the policy of the Shōgun. A decree had just been issued prohibiting the peasantry from exercising themselves with sword-play, and from wearing swords. Of this he says: "Perhaps this decree may have been issued on the supposition that Japan is naturally impregnable and defended on all sides. But when she receives insult from a foreign country, it may become necessary to call on the militia. And who knows that men of extraordinary military genius, like Toyotomi,[1] will not again appear among the lower classes?"

[1] Toyotomi Hidéyoshi, a peasant boy, rose from the position of a groom to be the actual ruler of Japan during the Middle Ages. He it was who in 1587 issued a decree of banishment against the Christian missionaries in Japan. He is called Faxiba in the writings of these missionaries, and in Japan he is frequently spoken of as Taiko Sama, a title, not a name; but a title that, used alone, refers always to him. For further account of his life, see Griffis, *Mikado's Empire*, book i., chap. xxiv.

He ends his memorial with this warning: " Should the Shōgun's court, and the military class in general, persist in the present oppressive way of government, Heaven will visit this land with still greater calamities. If this circumstance is not clearly kept in view, the consequence may be civil disturbance. I, therefore, beseech that the instructions of the glorious founder of the dynasty be acted upon; that simplicity and frugality be made the guiding principle of administration; and that a general amnesty be proclaimed, thereby complying with the will of Heaven and placating the people. Should these humble suggestions of mine be acted upon, prospective calamities will fly before the light of virtue. Whether the country is to be safe or not depends upon whether the administration is carried on with mercy or not. What I pray for is, that the country may enjoy peace and tranquillity, that the harvest may be plentiful, and that the people may be happy and prosperous."

One is able to see, by this rather remarkable document, that the peasants of Japan, though frequently almost crushed by the heavy burdens of taxation, do not, even in the most grinding poverty, lose entirely that independence of thought and of action which is characteristic of their nation. They do not consider themselves as a servile class, nor their military rulers as beyond criticism or reproach, but are ready to speak boldly for their rights whenever an opportunity occurs. There is a pathetic story, told in Mitford's "Tales of Old Japan," of a peasant, the head-man of his village, who goes to Yedo to present to the Shōgun a complaint, on behalf of his fellow-villagers, of the extortions and exactions of his daimiō. He is unable to get any one to present his memorial to the Shōgun, so at last he stops the great lord's palanquin in the street, — an act in itself punishable with death, — and thrusts the paper forcibly into his hand. The petition is read, and his fellow-villagers saved from further oppression, but the head-man, for his daring, is condemned by his own daimiō to suffer death by crucifixion, — a fate which he meets with the same heroism with which he dared everything to save his fellows from suffering.

The peasant, though ignorant and oppressed, has not lost his manhood; has not become a slave or a serf, but clings to his rights, so far as he knows what they are; and is ready to hold his own against all comers, when the question in debate is one that appeals to his mind. The rulers of Japan have always the peasantry to reckon with when their ruling becomes unjust or oppressive. They cannot be cowed, though they may be misled for a time, and they form a conservative element that serves to hold in check too hasty rulers who would introduce new measures too quickly, and would be likely to find the new wine bursting the old bottles, as well as to prevent any rash extravagance in the way of personal expenditure on the part of government officials. The influence of this great class will be more and more felt as the new parliamentary institutions gain in power, and a more close connection is established between the throne and public opinion.

In considering this great héimin class, it is well to remember that the artisans, who form so large a part of it, are also the artists who have made the reputation of Japan, in Europe and America, as one of the countries where art and the love of beauty in form and color are still instinct with life. The Japanese artisan works with patient toil, and with the skill and originality of the artist, to produce something that shall be individual and his own; not simply to make, after a pattern, some utensil or ornament for which he cares nothing, so long as a purchaser can be found for it, or an employer can be induced to pay him money for making it. It seems as easy for the Japanese to make things pretty and in good taste, even when they are cheap and only used by the poorer people, as it is for American mills and workers to turn out endless varieties of attempts at decoration, — all so hideous that a poor person must be content, either to be surrounded by the worst possible taste, or to purchase only such furnishings and utensils as are entirely without decoration of any kind. "Cheap" and "nasty" have come to be almost synonymous words with us, for the reason that taste in decoration is so rare that it commands a monopoly price, and can only be procured by the wealthy. In Japan this is not the case, for the cheapest of things may be found in graceful and artistic designs, — indeed can hardly be found in any designs that are not graceful and artistic; and the poorest and commonest of the people may have about them the little things that go to cultivate the æsthetic part of human nature. It was not the costly art of Japan that interested me the most, although that is, of course, the most wonderful proof of the capacity and patience of individuals among this héimin class: but it was the common, cheap, every-day art that meets one at every turn; the love for the beautiful, in both nature and art, that belongs to the common coolie as well as to the nobleman. The cheap prints, the blue and white towels, the common teacups and pots, the great iron kettles in use over the fire in the farmhouse kitchen, — all these are things as pretty and tasteful in their way as the rich crêpes, the silver incense burners, the delicate porcelain, and the elegant lacquer that fill the storehouse of the daimiō; and they show, much more conclusively than these costlier things, the universal sense of beauty among the people.

The artisan works at his home, helped less often by hired laborers than by his own children, who learn the trade of their father; and his house, though small, is clean and tasteful, with its soft mats, its dainty tea service, its little hanging scroll upon the walls, and its vase of gracefully arranged flowers in the corner; for flowers, even in winter and in the great city of Tōkyō, are so cheap that they are never beyond the reach of the poorest. In homes that seem to the foreign mind utterly lacking in the comforts and even the necessities of life, one finds the few furnishings and utensils beautiful in shape and decoration; and the money that in this country must be spent in beds, tables, and chairs can be used for the purchase of *kakémonos*, flowers, and vases, and for various gratifications of the æsthetic taste. Hence it is that the Japanese laborer, who lives on a daily wage which would reduce an American or European to the verge of starvation, finds both time and money for the cultivation of that sense of beauty which is too often crushed completely out of the lower classes by the burdens of this nineteenth century civilization which they bear upon their shoulders. To the Japanese, the "life is more than meat," it is beauty as well; and this love of beauty has upon him a civilizing and refining effect, and makes him in many ways the superior of the American day-laborer.

The peasants and farmers of Japan, thrifty and hard-working as they are, are not by any means a prosperous class. As one passes into the country districts from the large cities, there seems to be a conspicuous dearth of neat, pleasant homes, — a lack of the comforts and necessities of life such as are enjoyed by city people. The rich farmers are scarce, and the laborers in the rice-fields hardly earn, from days of hardest toil with the rudest implements, the little that will provide for their families. In the face of heavy taxes, the incessant toil, the frequent floods of late years, and the threatening famine, one would expect the poor peasants to be a most discouraged and unhappy class. That all this toil and anxiety does wear on them is no doubt true, but the laborers are always ready to bear submissively whatever comes, and are always hopeful and ready to enjoy life again in happier times. The life in the cities tempts them sometimes to exchange their daily labor for the excitement of life as *jinrikisha* men; but in any case they will be perfectly independent, and ask no man for their daily rations.

Although there is much poverty, there are few or no beggars in Japan, for both strong and weak find each some occupation that brings the little pittance required to keep soul and body together, and gives to all enough to make them light-hearted, cheerful, and even happy. From the rich farmer, whose many acres yield enough to provide for a home of luxury quite as fine as the city homes, to the poor little vender of sticks of candy, around whose store the children flock like bees with their rin and sen, all seem independent, contented, and satisfied with their lot in life.

The religious beliefs of old Japan are stronger to-day among the country people than among the dwellers in cities. And they are still willing to give of their substance for the aid of the dying faiths to which they cling, and to undertake toilsome pilgrimages to obtain some longed-for blessing from the gods whom they serve. A great Buddhist temple is being built in Kyōtō to-day, from the lofty ceiling of which hangs a striking proof of the devotion of some of the peasant women to the Buddhist faith. The whole temple, with its immense curved roof, its vast proportions, and its marvelous wood carvings, has been built by offerings of labor, money, and materials made by the faithful. The great timbers were given and brought to the spot by the countrymen; and the women, wishing to have some part in the sacred work, cut off their abundant hair, a beauty perhaps more prized by the Japanese women than by those of other countries, and from the material thus obtained they twisted immense cables, to be used in drawing the timbers from the mountains to the site of the temple. The great black cables hang in the unfinished temple to-day, a sign of the devotion of the women who spared not their chief ornament in the service of the gods in whom they still believe. And a close scrutiny of these touching offerings shows that the glossy black locks of the young women are mingled with the white hairs of those who, by this offering, hope to make sure of a quick and easy departure from a life already near its close.

All along the Tōkaidō, the great road from Tōkyō to Kyōto, in the neighborhood of some holy place, or in the district around the great and sacred Fuji, the mountain so much beloved and honored in Japanese art, will be seen bands of pilgrims slowly walking along the road, their worn and soiled white garments telling of many days' weary march. Their large hats shield them from the sun and the rain, and the pieces of matting slung over their backs serve them for beds to sleep on, when they take shelter for the night in rude huts. The way up the great mountain of Fuji is lined with these pilgrims; for to attain its summit, and worship there the rising sun, is believed to be the means of obtaining some special blessing. Among these religious devotees, in costumes not unlike those of the men, under the same large hat and coarse matting, old women often are seen, their aged faces belying their apparent vigor of body, as they walk along through miles and miles of country, jingling their bells and holding their rosaries until they reach the shrine, where they may ask some special blessing for their homes, or fulfill some vow already made.

Journeying through rural Japan, one is impressed by the important part played by women in the various bread-winning industries. In the village homes, under the heavily thatched roofs, the constant struggle against poverty and famine will not permit the women to hold back, but they enter bravely into all the work of the men. In the rice-field the woman works side by side with the man, standing all day up to her knees in mud, her dress tucked up and her lower limbs encased in tight-fitting, blue cotton trousers, planting, transplanting, weeding, and turning over the evil-smelling mire, only to be distinguished from her husband by her broader belt tied in a bow behind. In mountain regions we meet the women climbing the steep mountain roads, pruning-hook in hand, after wood for winter fires; or descending, towards night, carrying a load that a donkey need not be ashamed of, packed on a frame attached to the shoulders, or poised lightly upon a straw mat upon the head. There is one village near Kyōto, Yasé by name, at the base of Hiyéi Zan, the historic Buddhist stronghold, where the women attain a stature and muscular development quite unique among the pigmy population of the island empire. Strong, jolly, red-cheeked women they are, showing no evidence of the shrinking away with the advance of old age that is characteristic of most of their countrywomen. With their tucked-up *kimonos* and blue cotton trousers, they stride up and down the mountain, carrying the heaviest and most unwieldy of burdens as lightly and easily as the ordinary woman carries her baby. My first acquaintance with them was during a camping expedition upon the sacred mountain. I myself was carried up the ascent by two small, nearly naked, finely tattooed and moxa-scarred men; but my baggage, consisting of two closely packed hampers as large as ordinary steamer trunks, was lifted lightly to the heads of these feminine porters, and, poised on little straw pads, carried easily up the narrow trail, made doubly difficult by low-hanging branches, to the camp, a distance of three or four miles. From among these women of Yasé, on account of their remarkable physical development, have been chosen frequently the nurses for the imperial infants; an honor which the Yasé villagers duly appreciate, and which makes them bear themselves proudly among their less favored neighbors.

In other parts of the country, in the neighborhood of Nikkō, for instance, the care of the horses, mild little pack-mares that do much of the burden-bearing in those mountains, is mainly in the hands of the women. At Nikkō, when we would hire ponies for a two days' expedition to Yumoto, a little, elderly woman was the person with whom our bargains were made; and a close bargainer she proved to be, taking every advantage that lay in her power. When the caravan was ready to start, we found that, though each saddle-horse had a male groom in attendance, the pack-ponies on which our baggage was carried were led by pretty little country girls of twelve or fourteen, their bright black eyes and red cheeks contrasting pleasantly with the blue handkerchiefs that adorned their heads; their slender limbs encased in blue cotton, and only their red sashes giving any hint of the fact that they belonged to the weaker sex. As we journeyed up the rough mountain roads, the little girls kept along easily with the rest of the party; leading their meek, shock-headed beasts up the slippery log steps, and passing an occasional greeting with some returning pack-train, in which the soft black eyes and bits of red about the costume of the little grooms showed that they, too, were mountain maidens, returning fresh and happy after a two days' tramp through the rocky passes.

In the districts where the silkworm is raised, and the silk spun and woven, the women play a most important part in this productive industry. The care of the worms and of the cocoons falls entirely upon the women, as well as the spinning of the silk and the weaving of the cloth. It is almost safe to say that this largest and most productive industry of Japan is in the hands of the women; and it is to their care and skill that the silk product of the islands is due. In the silk districts one finds the woman on terms of equality with the man, for she is an important factor in the wealth-producing power of the family, and is thus able to make herself felt as she cannot when her work is inferior to that of the men. As a farmer, as a groom, or as a porter, a woman is and must remain an inferior, but in the care of the silkworms, and all the tasks that belong to silk culture, she is the equal of the stronger sex.

Then, again, in the tea districts, the tea plantations are filled with young girls and old women, their long sleeves held back by a band over the shoulder, and a blue towel gracefully fastened over their heads to keep off the sun and the dust. They pick busily away at the green, tender leaves, which will soon be heated and rolled by strong men over the charcoal fire. The occupation is an easy one, only requiring care in the selection of leaves to be picked, and can be performed by young girls and old women, who gather the glossy leaves in their big baskets, while chatting to each other over the gossip and news of the day.

In the hotels, both in the country and the city, women play an important part. The attendants are usually sweet-faced, prettily dressed girls, and frequently the proprietor of the hotel is a woman. My first experience of a Japanese hotel was at Nara, anciently the capital of Japan, and now a place of resort because of its fine old temples, its Dai Butsu, and its beautiful deer park. The day's ride in *jinrikisha* from Ōsaka had brought our party in very tired, only to find that the hotel to which we had telegraphed for rooms was already filled to overflowing by a daimiō and his suite. Not a room could be obtained, and we were at last obliged to walk some distance, for we had dismissed our tired *jinrikisha* men, to a hotel in the village, of which we knew nothing. What with fatigue and disappointment, we were not prepared to view the unknown hotel in a very rosy light; and when our guide pointed to a small gate leading into a minute, damp courtyard, we were quite convinced that the hardships of travel in Japan were now about to begin; but disappointment gave way to hope, when we were met at the door by a buxom landlady, whose smile was in itself a refreshment. Although we had little in the way of language in common, she made us feel at home at once, took us to her best room, sent her blooming and prettily dressed daughters to bring us tea and whatever other refreshments the mysterious appetite of a foreigner might require, and altogether behaved toward us in such motherly fashion that fatigue and gloom departed forthwith, leaving us refreshed and cheerful. Soon we began to feel rested, and our kind friend, seeing this, took us upon a tour around the house, in which room after room, spotless, empty, with shining woodwork and softest of mats, showed the good housekeeping of our hostess. A little garden in the centre of the house, with dwarf trees, moss-covered stones, and running water, gave it an air of coolness on the hot July day that was almost deceptive; and the spotless washroom, with its great stone sink, its polished brass basins, its stone well-curb, half in and half out of the house, was cool and clean and refreshing merely to look at. A two days' stay in this hotel showed that the landlady was the master of the house. Her husband was about the house constantly, as were one or two other men, but they all worked under the direction of the energetic head of affairs. She it was who managed everything, from the cooking of the meals in the kitchen to the filling and heating of the great bath-tub into which the guests were invited to enter every afternoon, one after the other, in the order of their rank. On the second night of my stay, at a late hour, when I supposed that the whole house had retired to rest, I crept softly out of my room to try to soothe the plaintive wails of my dog, who was complaining bitterly that he was made to sleep in the wood-cellar instead of in his mistress's room, as his habit had always been. As I stole quietly along, fearing lest I should arouse the sleeping house, I heard the inquiring voice of my landlady sound from the bath-room, the door of which stood wide open. Afraid that she would think me in mischief if I did not show myself, I went to the door, to find her, after her family was safely stowed away for the night, taking her ease in the great tub of hot water, and so preparing herself for a sound, if short, night's sleep. She accepted my murmured *Inu* (dog) as an excuse, and graciously dismissed me with a smile, and I returned to my room feeling safe under the vigilant care that seemed to guard the house by night as well as by day. I have seen many Japanese hotels and many careful landladies since, but no one among them all has made such an impression as my pleasant hostess at Nara.

Not only hotels, but little tea-houses all through Japan, form openings for the business abilities of women, both in country and city. Wherever you go, no matter how remote the district or how rough the road, at every halting point you find a little tea-house. Sometimes it is quite an extensive restaurant, with several rooms for the entertainment of guests, and a regular kitchen where fairly elaborate cooking can be done; sometimes it is only a rough shelter, at one end of which water is kept boiling over a charcoal brazier, while at the other end a couple of seats, covered with mats or a scarlet blanket or two, serve as resting-places for the patrons of the establishment. But whatever the place is, there will be one woman or more in attendance; and if you sit down upon the mats, you will be served at once with tea, and later, should you require more, with whatever the establishment can afford, — it may be only a slice of watermelon, or a hard pear; it may be eels on rice, vermicelli, egg soup, or a regular dinner, should the tea-house be one of the larger and more elaborately appointed ones. When the feast is over, the refreshments you have especially ordered are paid for in the regular way; but for the tea and sweetmeats offered, for which no especial charge is made, you are expected to leave a small sum as a present. In the less aristocratic resting-places, a few cents for each person is sufficient to leave on the waiter with the empty cups of tea, for which loud and grateful thanks will be shouted out to the returning party.

In the regular inn, the *chadai*[1] amounts to several dollars, for a party remaining any time, and it is supposed to pay for all the extra services and attention bestowed on guests by the polite host and hostess and the servants in attendance. The *chadai*, done up neatly in paper, with the words *On chadai* written on it, is given with as much formality as any present in Japan. The guest claps his hands to summon the maid. When it is heard, for the thin paper walls of a Japanese house let through every noise, voices from all sides will shout out *Hē'-hē'*, or *Hai*, which means that you have been heard, and understood. Presently a maid will softly open your door, and with head low down will ask what you wish. You tell her to summon the

[1] *Chadai* is, literally, "money for tea," and is equivalent to our tips to the waiters and porters at hotels. The *chadai* varies with the wealth and rank of the guests, the duration of the stay, and the attention which has been bestowed. *On* is the honorific placed before the word in writing.

landlord. In a few moments he appears, and you push the *chadai* to him, making some conventional self-depreciating speech, as, "You have done a great deal for our comfort, and we wish to give you this *ehadai*, though it is only a trifle." The landlord, with every expression of surprise, will bow down to the ground with thanks, raising the small package to his head in token of acceptance and gratitude, and will murmur in low tones how little he has done for the comfort of his guests; and then, the self-depreciation and formal words of thanks on his side being ended, he will finally go down stairs to see how much he has gotten. But, whether more or less than he had expected, nothing but extreme gratitude and politeness appears on his face as he presents a fan, confectionery, or some trifle, as a return for the *chadai*, and speeds the parting guests with his lowest bow and kindliest smile, after having seen to every want that could be attended to.

Once, at Nikkō, I started with a friend for a morning walk to a place described in the guide-book. The day was hot and the guide-book hazy, and we lost the road to the place for which we had set out, but found ourselves at last in a beautiful garden, with a pretty lake in its centre, a little red-lacquered shrine reflected in the lake, and a tea-house hospitably open at one side. The teakettle was boiling over the little charcoal fire; melons, eggs, and various unknown comestibles were on the little counter; but no voice bade us welcome as we approached, and when we sat down on the edge of the piazza, we could see no one within the house. We waited, however, for the day was hot, and time is not worth much in rural Japan. Pretty soon a small, wizened figure made its appearance in the distance, hurrying and talking excitedly as it came near enough to see two foreign ladies seated upon the piazza. Many bows and profuse apologies were made by the little old woman, who seemed to be the solitary occupant of the pretty garden, and who had for the moment deserted her post to do the day's marketing in the neighboring village. The apologies having been smilingly received, the old lady set herself to the task of making her guests comfortable. First she brought two tumblers of water, cold as ice, from the spring that gushed out of a great rock in the middle of the little lake. Then she retired behind a screen and changed her dress, returning speedily to bring us tea. Then she retreated to her diminutive kitchen, and presently came back smiling, bearing eight large raw potatoes on a tray. These she presented to us with a deep bow, apparently satisfied that she had at last brought us something we would be sure to like. We left the potatoes behind us when we went away, and undoubtedly the old lady is wondering still over the mysterious ways of the foreigners, as we are over those of the Japanese tea-house keepers.

One summer, when I was spending a week at a Japanese hotel at quite a fashionable seaside resort, I became interested in a little old woman who visited the hotel daily, carrying, suspended by a yoke from her shoulders, two baskets of fruit, which she sold to the guests of the hotel. As I was on the ground floor, and my room was, in the daytime, absolutely without walls on two sides, she was my frequent visitor, and, for the sake of her pleasant ways and cheerful smiles, I bought enough hard pears of her to have given the colic to an elephant. One day, after her visit to me, as I was sitting upon the matted and roofed square that served me for a room, my eye wandered idly toward the bathing beach, and, under the slight shelter where the bathers were in the habit of depositing their sandals and towels, I spied the well-known yoke and fruit baskets, as well as a small heap of blue cotton garments that I knew to be the clothing of the little fruit-vender. She had evidently taken a moment when trade was slack to enjoy a dip in the soft, blue, summer sea. Hardly had I made up my mind as to the meaning of the fruit baskets and the clothing, when our little friend herself emerged from the sea and, sitting down on a bench, proceeded to rub herself off with the small but artistically decorated blue towel that every peasant in Japan has always with him, however lacking he may be in all other appurtenances of the toilet. As she sat there, placidly rubbing away, a friend of the opposite sex made his appearance on the scene. I watched to see what she would do, for the Japanese code of etiquette is quite different from ours in such a predicament. She continued her employment until he was quite close, showing no unseemly haste, but continuing her polishing off in the same leisurely manner in which she had begun it; then at the proper moment she rose from her seat, bowed profoundly, and smilingly exchanged the greetings proper for the occasion, both parties apparently unconscious of any lack in the toilet of the lady. The male friend then passed on about his business; the little woman completed her toilet without further interruptions, shouldered her yoke, and jogged cheerfully on to her home in the little village, a couple of miles away.

As one travels through rural Japan in summer and sees the half-naked men, women, and children that pour out from every village on one's route and surround the *kuruma* at every stopping place, one sometimes wonders whether there is in the country any real civilization, whether these half-naked people are not more savage than civilized; but when one finds everywhere good hotels, scrupulous cleanliness in all the appointments of toilet and table, polite and careful service, honest and willing performance of labor bargained for, together with the gentlest and pleasantest of manners, even on the part of the gaping crowd that shut out light and air from the traveling foreigner who rests for a moment at the village inn, one is forced to reconsider a judgment formed only upon one peculiarity of the national life, and to conclude that there is certainly a high type of civilization in Japan, though differing in many important particulars from our own. A careful study of the Japanese ideas of decency, and frequent conversation with refined and intelligent Japanese ladies upon this subject, has led me to the following conclusion. According to the Japanese standard, any exposure of the person that is merely incidental to health, cleanliness, or convenience in doing necessary work, is perfectly modest and allowable; but an exposure, no matter how slight, that is simply for show, is in the highest degree indelicate. In illustration of the first part of this conclusion, I would refer to the open bath-houses, the naked laborers, the exposure of the lower limbs in wet weather by the turning up of the *kimono*, the entirely nude condition of the country children in summer, and the very slight clothing that even adults regard as necessary about the house or in the country during the hot season. In illustration of the last part, I would mention the horror with which many Japanese ladies regard that style of foreign dress which, while covering the figure completely, reveals every detail of the form above the waist, and, as we say, shows off to advantage a pretty figure. To the Japanese mind it is immodest to want to show off a pretty figure. As for the ball-room costumes, where neck and arms are freely exposed to the gaze of multitudes, the Japanese woman, who would with entire composure take her bath in the presence of others, would be in an agony of shame at the thought of appearing in public in a costume so indecent as that worn by many respectable American and European women. Our judgment would indeed be a hasty one, should we conclude that the sense of decency is wanting in the Japanese as a race, or that the women are at all lacking in the womanly instinct of modesty. When the point of view from which they regard these matters is once obtained, the apparent inconsistencies and incongruities are fully explained, and we can do justice to our Japanese sister in a matter in regard to which she is too often cruelly misjudged.

There seems no doubt at all that among the peasantry of Japan one finds the women who have the most freedom and independence. Among this class, all through the country, the women, though hard-worked and possessing few comforts, lead lives of intelligent, independent labor, and have in the family positions as respected and honored as those held by women in America. Their lives are fuller and happier than those of the women of the higher classes, for they are themselves bread-winners, contributing an important part of the family revenue, and they are obeyed and respected accordingly. The Japanese lady, at her marriage, lays aside her independent existence to become the subordinate and servant of her husband and parents-in-law, and her face, as the years go by, shows how much she has given up, how completely she has sacrificed herself to those about her. The Japanese peasant woman, when she marries, works side by side with her husband, finds life full of interest outside of the simple household work, and, as the years go by, her face shows more individuality, more pleasure in life, less suffering and disappointment, than that of her wealthier and less hard-working sister.

CHAPTER X.

LIFE IN THE CITIES.

THE great cities of Japan afford remarkable opportunities for seeing the life of the common people, for the little houses and shops, with their open fronts, reveal the *penetralia* in a way not known in our more secluded homes. The employment of the merchant being formerly the lowest of respectable callings, one does not find even yet in Japan many great stores or a very high standard of business morality, for the business of the country was left in the hands of those who were too stupid or too unambitious to raise themselves above that social class. Hence English and American merchants, who only see Japan from the business side, continually speak of the Japanese as dishonest, tricky, and altogether unreliable, and greatly prefer to deal with the Chinese, who have much of the business virtue that is characteristic of the English as a nation. Only within a few years have the samurai, or indeed any one who was capable of figuring in any higher occupation in life, been willing to adopt the calling of the merchant; but many of the abler Japanese of to-day have begun to see that trade is one of the most important factors of a nation's well-being, and that the business of buying and selling, if wisely and honestly done, is an employment that nobody need be ashamed to enter. There are in Japan a few great merchants whose word may be trusted, and whose obligations will be fulfilled with absolute honesty; but a large part of the buying and selling is still in the hands of mercantile freebooters, who will take an advantage wherever it is possible to get one, in whose morality honesty has no place, and who have not yet discovered the efficacy of that virtue simply as a matter of policy. Their trade, conducted in a small way upon small means, is more of the nature of a game, in which one person is the winner and the other the loser, than a fair exchange, in which both parties obtain what they want. It is the mediæval, not the modern idea of business, that is still held among Japanese merchants. With them, trade is a warfare between buyer and seller, in which every man must take all possible advantage for himself, and it is the lookout of the other party if he is cheated.

In Tōkyō, the greatest and most modernized of the cities of the empire, the shops are not the large city stores that one sees in European and American cities, but little open-fronted rooms, on the edge of which one sits to make one's purchases, while the proprietor smiles and bows and dickers; setting his price by the style of his customer's dress, or her apparent ignorance of the value of the desired article. Some few large dry-goods stores there are, where prices are set and dickering is unnecessary; and in the *kwankoba*, or bazaars, one may buy almost anything needed by Japanese of all classes, from house furnishings to foreign hats, at prices plainly marked upon them, and from which there is no variation. But one's impression of the state of trade in Japan is, that it is still in a very primitive and undeveloped condition, and is surprisingly behind the other parts of Japanese civilization.

The shopping of the ladies of the large

yashikis and of wealthy families is done mostly in the home; for all the stores are willing at any time, on receiving an order, to send up a clerk with a bale of crêpes, silks, and cottons tied to his back, and frequently towering high above his head as he walks, making him look like the proverbial ant with a grain of wheat. He sets his great bundle carefully down on the floor, opens the enormous *furushiki*, or bundle handkerchief, in which it is enveloped, and takes out roll after roll of silk or chintz, neatly done up in paper or yellow cotton. With infinite patience, he waits while the merits of each piece are examined and discussed, and if none of his stock proves satisfactory, he is willing to come again with a new set of wares, knowing that in the end purchases will be made sufficient to cover all his trouble.

The less aristocratic people are content to go to the stores themselves; and the business streets of a Japanese city, such as the Ginza in Tōkyō, are full of women, young and old, as well as merry children, who enjoy the life and bustle of the stores. Like all things else in Japan, shopping takes plenty of time. At Mitsui's, the largest silk store in Tōkyō, one will see crowds of clerks sitting upon the matted floors, each with his *soroban*, or adding machine, by his side; and innumerable small boys, who rush to and fro, carrying armfuls of fabrics to the different clerks, or picking up the same fabrics after the customer who has called for them has departed. The store appears, to the foreign eye, to be simply a roofed and matted platform upon which both clerks and customers sit. This platform is screened from the street by dark blue cotton curtains or awnings hung from the low projecting eaves of the heavy roof. As the customers take their seats, either on the edge of the platform, or, if they have come on an extended shopping bout, upon the straw mat of the platform itself, a small boy appears with tea for the party; an obsequious clerk greets them with the customary salutations of welcome, pushes the charcoal brazier toward them, that they may smoke, or warm their hands, before proceeding to business, and then waits expectantly for the name of the goods that his customers desire to see. When this is given, the work begins; the little boys are summoned, and are soon sent off to the great fire-proof warehouse, which stands with heavy doors thrown open, on the other side of the platform, away from the street. Through the doorway one can see endless piles of costly stuffs stored safely away, and from these piles the boys select the required fabric, loading themselves down with them so that they can barely stagger under the weights that they carry. As the right goods are not always brought the first time, and as, moreover, there is an endless variety in the colors and patterns in even one kind of silk, there is always plenty of time for watching the busy scene, — for sipping tea, or smoking a few whiffs from the tiny pipes that so many Japanese, both men and women, carry always with them. When the purchase is at last made, there is still some time to be spent by the customer in waiting until the clerk has made an abstruse calculation upon his *soroban*, the transaction has been entered in the books of the firm, and a long bill has been written and stamped, and handed to her with the bundle. During her stay in the store, the foreign customer, making her first visit to the place, is frequently startled by loud shouts from the whole staff of clerks and small boys, — outcries so sudden, so simultaneous, and so stentorian, that she cannot rid herself of the idea that something terrible is happening every time that they occur. She soon learns, however, that these manifestations of energy are but the way in which the Japanese merchant speeds the departing purchaser, and that the apparently inarticulate shouts are but the formal phrase, " Thanks for your continued favors," which is repeated in a loud tone by every employee in the store whenever a customer departs. When she herself is at last ready to leave, a chorus of yells arises, this time for her benefit; and as she skips into the *jinrikisha* and is whirled away, she hears continued the busy hum of voices, the clattering of *sorobans*, the thumping of the bare feet of the heavily laden boys, and the loud shouts of thanks with which departing guests are honored.

There is less pomp and circumstance about the smaller stores, for all the goods are within easy reach, and the shops for household utensils and chinaware seem to have nearly the whole stock in trade piled up in front, or even in the street itself.

Many such little places are the homes of the people who keep them. And at the back are rooms, which serve for dwelling rooms, opening upon well-kept gardens. The whole work of the store is often attended to by the proprietor, assisted by his wife and family, and perhaps one or two apprentices. Each of the workers, in turn, takes an occasional holiday, for there is no day in the Japanese calendar when the shops are all closed; and even New Year's Day, the great festival of the year, finds most of the stores open. Yet the dwellers in these little homes, living almost in the street, and in the midst of the bustle and crowd and dust of Tōkyō, have still time to enjoy their holidays and their little gardens, and have more pleasure and less hard work than those under similar circumstances in our own country.

The stranger visiting any of the great Japanese cities is surprised by the lack of large stores and manufactories, and often wonders where the beautiful lacquer work and porcelains are made, and where the gay silks and crêpes are woven. There are no large establishments where such things are turned out by wholesale. The delicate vases, the bronzes, and the silks are often made in humblest homes, the work of one or two laborers with rudest tools. There are no great manufactories to be seen, and the bane of so many cities, the polluting factory smoke, never rises over the cities of Japan. The hard, confining factory life, with its never-ceasing roar of machinery, bewildering the minds and intellects of the men who come under its deadening influences, until they become scarcely more than machines themselves, is a thing as yet almost unknown in Japan. The life of the *jinrikisha* man even, hard and comfortless as it may seem to run all day like a horse through the crowded city streets, is one that keeps him in the fresh air, under the open sky, and quickens his powers both of body and mind. To the poor in Japanese cities is never denied the fresh air and sunshine, green trees and grass; and the beautiful parks and gardens are found everywhere, for the enjoyment of even the meanest and lowest.

On certain days in the month, in different sections of the city, are held night festivals near temples, and many shopkeepers take the opportunity to erect temporary booths, in which they so arrange their wares as to tempt the passers-by as they go to and fro. Very often there is a magnificent display of young trees, potted plants, and flowers, brought in from the country and ranged on both sides of the street. Here the gardeners make lively sales, as the displays are often fine in themselves, and show to a special advantage in the flaring torchlight. The eager venders, who do all they can to call the attention of the crowd to their wares, make many good bargains. The purchase requires skill on both sides, for flower men are proverbial in their high charges, asking often five and ten times the real value of a plant, but coming down in price almost immediately on remonstrance. You ask the price of a dwarf wistaria growing in a pot. The man answers at once, "Two dollars." "Two dollars!" you answer in surprise, "it is not worth more than thirty or forty cents." "Seventy-five, then," he will respond; and thus the buyer and seller approach nearer in price, until the bargain is struck somewhere near the first price offered. Price another plant and there would be the same process to go over again; but as the evening passes, prices go lower and lower, for the distances that the plants have been brought are great, and the labor of loading up and carrying back the heavy pots is a weary one, and when the last customer has departed the merchants must work late into the night to get their wares safely home again.

But beside the flower shows, there are long rows of booths, which, with the many visitors who throng the streets, make a gay and lively scene. So dense is the crowd that it is with difficulty one can push through on foot or in *jinrikisha*. The darkness is illuminated by torches, whose weird flames flare and smoke in the wind, and shine down upon the little sheds which line both sides of the road, and contain so tempting a display of cheap toys and trinkets that not only the children, but their elders, are attracted by them. Some of the booths are devoted to dolls; others to toys of various kinds; still others to birds in cages, goldfish in globes, queer chirping insects in wicker baskets, pretty ornaments for the hair, fans, candies, and cakes of all sorts, roasted beans and peanuts, and other things too numerous to mention. The long line of stalls ends with booths, or tents, in which shows of dancing, jugglery, educated animals, and monstrosities, natural or artificial, may be seen for the moderate admission fee of two cents. Each of these shows is well advertised by the beating of drums, by the shouting of doorkeepers, by wonderful pictures on the outside to entice the passer-by, or even by an occasional brief lifting of the curtains which veil the scene from the crowd without, just long enough to afford a tantalizing glimpse of the wonders within. Great is the fascination to the children in all these things, and the little feet are never weary until the last booth is passed, and the quiet of neighboring streets, lighted only by wandering lanterns, strikes the home-returning party by its contrast with the light and noise of the festival. The supposed object of the expedition, the visit to the temple, has occupied but a small share of time and attention, and the little hands are filled with the amusing toys and trifles bought, and the little minds with the merry sights seen. Nor are those who remain at home forgotten, but the pleasure seekers who visit the fair carry away with them little gifts for each member of the family, and the *O miagé*, or present given on the return, is a regular institution of Japanese home life.[1]

By ten o'clock, when the crowds have dispersed and the purchasers have all gone home and gone to bed, the busy booth-keepers take down their stalls, pack up their wares, and disappear, leaving no trace of the night's gayeties to greet the morning sun.

Beside these evening shows, which occur monthly or oftener, there are also great festivals of the various gods, some celebrated annually, others at intervals of some years. These *matsuri* last for several days, and during that time the quarter of the city in which they occur seems entirely given over to festivity. The streets are gayly decorated with flags, and bright lanterns — all alike in design and color — are hung in rows from the low eaves of the houses. Young bamboo-trees set along the street, and decorated with bits of bright-colored tissue paper, are a frequent and ef-

[1] *O miagé* must be given, not only on the return from an evening of pleasure, but also on the return from a journey or pleasure trip of any kind. As a rule, the longer the absence, the finer and more costly must be the presents given on returning.

fective accompaniment of these festivals, and here and there throughout the district are set up high stands, on the tops of which musicians with squeaky flutes, and drums of varying calibre, keep up a din more festive than harmonious. It takes a day or two for the rejoicings to get fully under way, but by the second or third day the fun is at its height, and the streets are thronged with merrymakers. A great deal of labor and strength, as well as ingenuity, is spent in the construction of enormous floats, or *dashi*, lofty platforms of two stories, either set on wheels and drawn by black bullocks or crowds of shouting men, or carried by poles on men's shoulders. Upon the first floor of these great floats is usually a company of dancers, or mummers, who dance, attitudinize, or make faces for the amusement of the crowds that gather along their route; while up above, an effigy of some hero in Japanese history, or the figure of some animal or monster, looks down unmoved upon the absurdities below. Each *dashi* is attended, not only by the men who draw it, but by companies of others in some uniform costume; and sometimes graceful professional dancing-girls are hired to march in the *matsuri* procession, or to dance upon the lofty *dashi*. At the time of the festivities which accompanied the promulgation of the Constitution, three days of jollification were held in Tōkyō, days of such universal fun and frolic that it will be known among the common people, to all succeeding generations, as the "Emperor's big *matsuri*." Every quarter of the city vied with every other in the production of gorgeous *dashi*, and the streets were gay with every conceivable variety of decoration, from the little red-and-white paper lanterns, that even the poorest hung before their houses, to the great evergreen arches, set with electric lights, with which the great business streets were spanned thickly from end to end. An evening walk through one of these thoroughfares was a sight to be remembered for a lifetime. The magnificent *dashi* represented all manner of quaint conceits. A great bivalve drawn by yelling crowds — which halted occasionally — opened and displayed between its shells a group of beautifully dressed girls, who danced one of the pantomimic dances of the country, accompanied by the twanging melodies of the *samisen*. Then slowly the great shell closed, once more the shouting crowds seized hold of the straining ropes, and the great bivalve with its fair freight was drawn slowly along through the gayly illuminated streets. Jimmu Tenno and other heroes of Japanese legend or history, each upon its lofty platform, a white elephant, and countless other subjects were represented in the festival cars sent forth by all the districts of the city to celebrate the great event.

Upon such festival occasions the shopkeeper does not put up his shutters and leave his place of business, but the open shop-fronts add much to the gay appearance of the street. There are no signs of business about, but the floor of the shop is covered with bright-red blankets; magnificent gilded screens form an imposing background to the little room; and seated on the floor are the shopkeeper, his family, and guests, eating, drinking tea, and smoking, as cosily as if all the world and his wife were not gazing upon the gay and homelike interior. Sometimes companies of dancers, or other entertainments furnished by the wealthier shopkeepers, will attract gaping crowds, who watch and block the street until the advance guard of some approaching *dashi* scatters them for a moment.

In Japan, as in other parts of the world, the country people are rather looked down upon by the dwellers in the city for their slowness of intellect, dowdiness of dress, and boorishness of manners; while the country people make fun of the fads and fashions of the city, and rejoice that they are not themselves the slaves of novelty, and especially of the foreign innovations that play so prominent a part in Japanese city life to-day. "The frog in the well knows not the great ocean," is the snub with which the Japanese cockney sets down Farmer Rice-Field's expressions of opinion; while the conservative countryman laughs at the foreign affectations of the Tōkyō man, and returns to his village with tales of the cookery of the capital: so extravagant is it that sugar is used in everything; it is even rumored that the Tōkyōites put sugar in their tea.

But while the country laughs and wonders at the city, nevertheless, in Japan as elsewhere, there is a constant crowding of the young life of the country into the livelier and more entertaining city. Tōkyō especially is the goal of every young countryman's ambition, and thither he goes to seek his fortune, finding, alas! too often, only the hard lot of the *jinrikisha* man, instead of the wealth and power that his country dreams had shown him.

The lower class women of the cities are in many respects like their sisters of the rural districts, except that they have less freedom than the country women in what the economists call "direct production." The wells and water tanks that stand at convenient distances along the streets of Tōkyō are frequently surrounded by crowds of women, drawing water, washing rice, and chattering merrily over their occupations. They meet and exchange ideas freely with each other and with the men, but they have not the diversity of labor that country life affords, confining themselves more closely to indoor and domestic work, and leaving the bread-winning more entirely to the men.

There are, however, occupations in the city for women, by which they may support themselves or their families. A good hair-dresser may make a handsome living; indeed, she does so well that it is proverbial among the Japanese that a hair-dresser's husband has nothing to do. Though professional tailors are mostly men, many women earn a small pittance in taking in sewing and in giving sewing lessons; and as instructors in the ceremonial tea, etiquette, music, painting, and flower arrangement, many women of the old school are able to earn an independence, though none of these occupations are confined to the women alone.

The business of hotel-keeping we have referred to in a previous chapter, and it is a well-known fact that unless a hotel-keeper has a capable wife, his business will not succeed. At present, all over Tōkyō, small restaurants, where food is served in the foreign style, are springing up, and these are usually conducted by a man and his wife who have at some time served as cook and waitress in a foreign family, and who conduct the business coöperatively and on terms of good-fellowship and equality. In these little eating-houses, where a well-cooked foreign dinner of from three to six courses is served for the moderate sum of thirty or forty cents, the man usually does the cooking, the woman the serving and handling of the money, until the time arrives when the profits of the business are sufficient to justify the hiring of more help. When this time comes, the labor is redistributed, the woman frequently taking upon herself the reception of the guests and the keeping of the accounts, while the hired help waits on the tables.

One important calling, in the eyes of many persons, especially those of the lower classes, is that of fortune-telling; and these guides in all matters of life, both great and small, are to be found in every section of the city. They are consulted on every important step by believing ones of all classes. An impending marriage, an illness, the loss of any valuable article, a journey about to be taken, — these are all subjects for the fortune-teller. He tells the right day of marriage, and says whether the fates of the two parties will combine well; gives clues to the causes of sudden illness, and information as to what has become of lost articles, and whether they will be recovered or not. Warned thus by the fortune-teller against evils that may happen, many ingenious expedients are resorted to, to avoid the ill foretold.

A man and his family were about to move from their residence to another part of the city. They sent to know if the fates were propitious to the change for all the family. The day and year of birth of each was told, and then the fortune-teller hunted up the various signs, and sent word that the direction of the new home was excellent for the good luck of the family as a whole, and the move a good one for each member of it except one of the sons; the next year the same move would be bad for the father. As the family could not wait two years before moving, it was decided that the change of residence should be made at once, but that the son should live with his uncle until the next year. The uncle's home was, however, inconveniently remote, and so the young man stayed as a visitor at his father's house for the remaining months of the year, after which he became once more a member of the household. Thus the inconvenience and the evil were both avoided.

Another story comes to my mind now of a dear old lady, the Go Inkyo Sama of a house of high rank, who late in life came to Tōkyō to live with her brother and his young and somewhat foreignized wife. The brother himself, while not a Christian, had little belief in the old superstitions of his people; his wife was a professing Christian. Soon after the old lady's arrival in Tōkyō, her sister-in-law fell ill, and before she had recovered her strength the children, one after another, came down with various diseases, which, though in no case fatal, kept the family in a state of anxiety for more than a year. The old lady was quite sure that there was some witchcraft or art-magic at work among her dear ones, and, after consulting the servants (for she knew that she could expect no sympathy in her plans from either her brother or his wife), she betook herself to a fortune-teller to discover through his means the causes of the illness in the family. The fortune-teller revealed to her the fact that two occult forces were at work bringing evil upon the house. One was the evil spirit of a spring or well that had been choked with stones, or otherwise obstructed in its flow, and that chose this way of bringing its afflictions to the attention of mortals.

The other was the spirit of a horse that had once belonged in the family, and that after death revenged itself upon its former masters for the hard service wherewith it had been made to serve. The only way in which these two powers could be appeased would be by finding the well, and removing the obstructions that choked it, and by erecting an image of the horse and offering to it cakes and other meat-offerings. The fortune-teller hinted, moreover, that for a consideration he might be able to afford material aid in the search for the well.

At this information Go Inkyo Sama was much perturbed, for further aid for her afflicted family seemed to require the use of money, and of that commodity she had very little, being mainly dependent upon her brother for support. She returned to her home and consulted the servants upon the matter; but though they quite agreed with her that something should be done, they had little capital to invest in the enterprises suggested by the fortune-teller. At last, the old lady went to her brother, but he only laughed at her well-meant attempts to help his family, and refused to give her money for such a purpose. She retired discouraged, but, urged by the servants, she decided to make a last appeal, this time to her sister-in-law, who must surely be moved by the evil that was threatening herself and her children. Taking some of the head servants with her, she went to her sister and presented the case. This was her last resort, and she clung to her forlorn hope longer than many would have done, the servants adding their arguments to her impassioned appeals, only to find out after all that the steadfast sister could not be moved, and that she would not propitiate the horse's spirit, or allow money to be used for such a purpose. She gave it up then, and sat down to await the fate of her doomed house, doubtless wondering much and sighing often over the foolish skepticism of her near relatives, and wishing that the rationalistic tendencies of the time would take a less dangerous form than the neglecting of the plainest precautions for life and health. The fate has not yet come, and now at last Go Inkyo Sama seems to have resigned herself to the belief that it has been averted from the heads of the dear ones by a power unknown to the fortune-teller.

Beside these callings, there are other employments which are not regarded as wholly respectable by either Japanese or foreigners. The *géisha ya*, or establishments where dancing-girls are trained, and let out by the day or evening to tea-houses or private parties, are usually managed by women. At these establishments little girls are taken, sometimes by contract with their parents, sometimes adopted by the proprietors of the house, and from very early youth are trained not only in the art of dancing, but are taught singing and *samisen*-playing, all the etiquette of serving and entertaining guests, and whatever else goes to make a girl charming to the opposite sex. When thoroughly taught, they form a valuable investment, and well repay the labor spent upon them, for a popular géisha commands a good price everywhere, and has her time overcrowded with engagements. A Japanese entertainment is hardly regarded as complete without géishas in attendance, and their dancing, music, and graceful service at supper form a charming addition to an evening of enjoyment at a tea-house. It is these géishas, too, who at *matsuri* are hired to march in quaint uniforms in the procession, or, borne aloft on great *dashi*, dance for the benefit of the admiring crowds.

The Japanese dances are charmingly graceful and modest; the swaying of the body and limbs, the artistic management of the flowing draperies, the variety of themes and costumes of the different dances, all go to make an entertainment by géishas one of the pleasantest of Japanese enjoyments. Sometimes, in scarlet and yellow robes, the dainty maidens imitate, with their supple bodies, the dance of the maple leaves as they are driven hither and thither in the autumn wind; sometimes, with tucked-up *kimonos* and jaunty red petticoats, they play the part of little country girls carrying their eggs to market in the neighboring village. Again, clad in armor, they simulate the warlike gestures and martial stamp of some of the old-time heroes; or, with whitened faces and hoary locks, they perform with rake and broom the dance of the good old man and old woman who play so prominent a part in Japanese pictures. And then, when the dance is over, and all are bewitched with their grace and beauty, they descend to the supper-room and ply their temporary employers with the *saké* bottle, laughing and jesting the while, until there is little wonder if the young men at the entertainment drink more than is good for them, and leave the tea-house at last thoroughly tipsy, and enslaved by the bright eyes and merry wits of some of the Hebes who have beguiled them through the evening.

The géishas unfortunately, though fair, are frail. In their system of education, manners stand higher than morals, and many a géisha gladly leaves the dancing in the tea houses to become the concubine of some wealthy Japanese or foreigner, thinking none the worse of herself for such a business arrangement, and going cheerfully back to her regular work, should her contract be unexpectedly ended. The géisha is not necessarily bad, but there is in her life much temptation to evil, and little stimulus to do right, so that, where one lives blameless, many go wrong, and drop below the margin of respectability altogether. Yet so fascinating, bright, and lively are these géishas that many of them have been taken by men of good position as wives, and are now the heads of the most respectable homes. Without true education or morals, but trained thoroughly in all the arts and accomplishments that please, — witty, quick at repartee, pretty, and always well dressed, — the géisha has proved a formidable rival for the demure, quiet maiden of good family, who can only give her husband an unsullied name, silent obedience, and faithful service all her life. The freedom of the present age, as shown in the chapter on "Marriage and Divorce," and as seen in the choice of such wives, has presented this great problem to the thinking women of Japan. If the wives of the leaders in Japan are to come from among such a class of women, something must be done, and done quickly, for the sake of the future of Japan; either to raise the standards of the men in regard to women, or to change the old system of education for girls. A liberal education, and more freedom in early life for women, has been suggested, and is now being tried, but the problem of the géisha and her fascination is a deep one in Japan.

Below the géisha in respectability stands the jōrō, or licensed prostitute. Every city in Japan has its disreputable quarter, where the various *jōrōya,* or licensed houses of prostitution, are situated. The supervision that the government exercises over these places is extremely rigid; the effort is made, by licensing and regulating them, to minimize the evils that must flow from them. The proprietors of the *jōrōya* do everything in their power to make their houses, grounds, and employees attractive, and, to the unsuspecting foreigner, this portion of the city seems often the pleasantest and most respectable. A jōrō need never be taken for a respectable woman, for her dress is distinctive, and a stay of a short time in Japan is long enough to teach even the most obtuse that the *obi,* or sash, tied in front instead of behind, is one of the badges of shame. But though the occupation of the jōrō is altogether disreputable,— though the prostitute quarter is the spot to which the police turn for information in regard to criminals and law-breakers, a sort of a trap into which, sooner or later, the offender against the law is sure to fall,— Japanese public opinion, though recognizing the evil as a great one, does not look upon the professional prostitute with the loathing which she inspires in Christian countries. The reason for this lies, not solely in the lower moral standards although it is true that sins of this character are regarded much more leniently in Japan than in England or America. The reason lies very largely in the fact that these women are seldom free agents. Many of them are virtually slaves, sold in childhood to the keepers of the houses in which they work, and trained, amid the surroundings of the *jōrōya*, for the life which is the only life they have ever known. A few may have sacrificed themselves freely but reluctantly for those whom they love, and by their revolting slavery may be earning the means to keep their dear ones from starvation or disgrace. Many are the Japanese romances that are woven about the virtuous *jōrō*, who is eventually rewarded by finding, even in the *jōrōya*, a lover who is willing to raise her again to a life of respectability, and make her a happy wife and the mother of children. Such stories must necessarily lower the standard of morals in regard to chastity, but in a country in which innocent romance has little room for development, the imagination must find its materials where it can. These *jōrōya* give employment to thousands of women throughout the country, but in few cases do the women seek that employment, and more openings in respectable directions, together with a change in public opinion securing to every woman the right to her own person, would tend to diminish the number of victims that these institutions yearly draw into their devouring current.

Innocent and reputable amusements are many and varied in the cities. We have already mentioned incidentally the theatre as one of the favorite diversions of the people; and though it has never been regarded as a very refined amusement, it has done and is doing much for the education of the lower classes in the history and spirit of former times. Regular plays were never performed in the presence of the Emperor and his court, or the Shōgun and his nobles, but the *No* dance was the only dramatic amusement of the nobility. This *No* is an ancient Japanese theatrical performance, more, perhaps, like the Greek drama than anything in our modern life. All the movements of the actors are measured and conventionalized, speech is a poetical recitative, the costumes are stiff and antique, masks are much used, and a chorus seated upon the stage chants audible comments upon the various situations. This alone, the most ancient and classical of Japanese theatrical performances, is considered worthy of the attention of the Emperor and the nobility, and takes the place with them of the more vulgar and realistic plays which delight common people.

The regular theatre preserves in many ways the life and costumes of old Japan, and the details of dress and scenery are most carefully studied. The actors are usually men, though there are "women theatres" in which all the parts are performed by women. In no case are the rôles taken by both sexes upon one stage. As the performances last all day, from ten or eleven in the forenoon until eight or nine in the evening, going to the theatre means much more than a few hours of entertainment after the day's work is over. A lunch and dinner, with innumerable light edibles between, go to make up the usual bill of fare for a day at the play, and tea-houses in the neighborhood of the theatre provide the necessary meals, a room to take them in, a resting-place between the acts, and whatever tea, cakes, and other refreshments may be ordered. These latter eatables are served by the attendants of the tea-house in the theatre boxes while the play is in progress, and the playgoers eat and smoke all day long through roaring farce or goriest tragedy.

Similar to the theatre in many ways are the public halls, where professional story-tellers, the *hanashika,* night after night, relate long stories to crowded audiences, as powerfully and vividly as the best trained elocutionist. Each gesture, and each modulation of the voice, is studied as carefully as are those of the actors. Many charming tales are told of old Japan, and even Western stories have found their way to these assemblies. A long story is often continued from night to night until finished. Unfortunately, the class of people who patronize these places is low, and the moral tone of some of the stories is pitched accordingly; but the best of the story-tellers — those who have talent and reputation — are often invited to come to entertainments given at private houses, to amuse a large company by their eloquence or mimicry.

This is a very favorite entertainment, and the *hanashika* has so perfected the art of imitation that he can change in a moment from the tones of a child to those of an old woman. Solemn and sad subjects are touched upon, as well as merry and bright things, and he never fails to make his audience weep or laugh, according to his theme, and well merits the applause he always receives at the end.

The *hanami*, or picnic to famous places to view certain flowers as they bloom in their season, though not belonging strictly to city life, forms one of the greatest of the pleasures of city people. The river Sumida, on which Tōkyō is situated, has lining its eastern shore for some miles the famous cherry-trees of Japan, with their large, double pink blossoms, and when, in April and May, these flowers are in their perfection, great crowds of sightseers flock to Mukōjima to enjoy the blossoms under the trees. The river is crowded with picnic parties in boats. Every tea-house along the banks is full of guests, and the little stalls and resting-places on the way find a quick sale for fruit, confectionery, and light lunches. *Saké* is often too freely imbibed by the merrymakers, whose flushed faces show, when returning homeward, how their day was spent. There is much quiet enjoyment, too, of the lovely blossoms, the broad, calm river, and the gayly dressed crowds. Hundreds and thousands of visitors crowd to the suburban places about Tōkyō, — to Uyéno Park for its cherry and peach blossoms, Kaméido for the plum and wistaria, Oji for its famous maple-trees, and many others, each noted for some special beauty. Dango Zaka has its own peculiar attraction, the famous chrysanthemum dolls. These ingenious figures are arranged so as to form tableaux, — scenes from history or fiction well known to all the people. They are of life size, and the faces, hands, and feet are made of some composition, and closely resemble life in every detail. But the curious thing in these tableaux is that the scenery, whether it be the representation of a waterfall, rocks, or bushes, the animals, and the dresses of the figures are made entirely of chrysanthemum twigs, leaves, and flowers, not cut and woven in, as at the first glance they seem to be, — so closely are the leaves and flowers bound together to make the flat surface of different objects, — but alive and growing on the plants. It is impossible to tell where the roots and stems are hidden, for nothing is visible but (for example) the white spray and greenish shadows of a waterfall, or the parti-colored figures in a young girl's dress. But, should it be the visitor's good fortune to watch the repairing of one of these lifelike images, he will find that the entire body is a frame woven of split bamboo, within which the plants are placed, their roots packed in damp earth and bound about with straw, while their leaves and flowers are pulled through the basket frame and woven into whatsoever pattern the artistic eye and skillful fingers of the gardener may select. A roof of matting shields each group from the sun by day, and a slight sprinkling every night serves to keep the plants fresh for nearly a month, and the flowers continue their blooming during that time, as calmly as if in perfectly natural positions. Each of the gardeners of the neighborhood has his own little show, containing several tableaux, the entrance to which is guarded by an officious gate-keeper, who shouts out the merits of his particular groups of figures, and forces his show-bills upon the passer-by, in the hope of securing the two sen admission fee which is required for each exhibit.

And so, amid the shopping, the festivals, the amusements of the great cities, the women find their lives varied in many ways. Their holidays from home duties are spent amid these enjoyments; and if they have not the out-of-door employments, the long walks up the mountains, the days spent in tea-picking, in harvesting, in all the varied work that comes to the country woman, the dwellers in the city have no lack of sights and sounds to amuse and interest them, and would not often care to exchange their lot for the freer and hardier life of the rustic.

CHAPTER XI.

DOMESTIC SERVICE.

To the foreigner, upon his arrival in Japan, the status of household servants is at first a source of much perplexity. There is a freedom in their relations with the families that they serve, that in this country would be regarded as impudence, and an independence of action that, in many cases, seems to take the form of direct disobedience to orders. From the steward of your household, who keeps your accounts, makes your purchases, and manages your affairs, to your *jinrikisha* man or groom, every servant in your establishment does what is right in his own eyes, and after the manner that he thinks best. Mere blind obedience to orders is not regarded as a virtue in a Japanese servant; he must do his own thinking, and, if he cannot grasp the reason for your order, that order will not be carried out. Housekeeping in Japan is frequently the despair of the thrifty

American housewife, who has been accustomed in her own country to be the head of every detail of household work, leaving to her servants only the mechanical labor of the hands. She begins by showing her Oriental help the work to be done, and just the way in which she is accustomed to having it done at home, and the chances are about one in a hundred that her servant will carry out her instructions. In the ninety-nine other cases, he will accomplish the desired result, but by means totally different from those to which the American housekeeper is accustomed. If the housewife is one of the worrying kind, who cares as much about the way in which the thing is done as about the accomplished result, the chances are that she will wear herself out in a fruitless endeavor to make her servants do things in her own way, and will, when she returns to America, assure you that Japanese servants are the most idle, stupid, and altogether worthless lot that it was ever her bad fortune to have to do with. But on the other hand, if the lady of the house is one who is willing to give general orders, and then sit down and wait until the work is done before criticising it, she will find that by some means or other the work will be accomplished and her desire will be carried out, provided only that her servants see a reason for getting the thing done. And as she finds that her domestics will take responsibility upon themselves, and will work, not only with their hands, but with the will and intellect in her service, she soon yields to their protecting and thoughtful care for herself and her interests, and, when she returns to America, is loud in her praises of the competence and devotion of her Japanese servants. Even in the treaty ports, where contact with foreigners has given to the Japanese attendants the silent and repressed air that we regard as the standard manner for a servant, they have not resigned their right of private judgment, but, if faithful and honest, seek the best good of their employer, even if his best good involves disobedience of his orders. This characteristic of the Japanese servant is aggravated when he is in the employment of foreigners, for the simple reason that he is apt to regard the foreigner as a species of imbecile, who must be cared for tenderly because he is quite incompetent to care for himself, but whose fancies must not be too much regarded. Of the relations of foreign employers and Japanese servants much might be said, but our business is with the position of the servants in a Japanese household.

Under the old feudal system, the servants of every family were its hereditary retainers, and from generation to generation desired no higher lot than personal service in the family to which they belonged. The principle of loyalty to the family interests was the leading principle in the lives of the servants, just as loyalty to the daimiō was the highest duty of the samurai. Long and intimate knowledge of the family history and traits of character rendered it possible for the retainer to work intelligently for his master, and do independently for him many things without orders. The servant in many cases knew his master and his master's interests as well as the master himself, or even better, and must act by the light of his own knowledge in cases where his master was ignorant or misinformed. One can easily see how ties of good-fellowship and sympathy would arise between masters and servants, how a community of interest would exist, so that the good of the master and his family would be the condition for the good of the servant and his family. In America, where the relation between servant and employer is usually a simple business arrangement, each giving certain specified considerations and nothing more, the relation of servant to master is shorn of all sentiment and affection; the servant's interests are quite apart from those of his employer, and his main object is to get the specified work done and obtain more time for himself, and sooner or later to leave the despised occupation of domestic service for some higher and more independent calling. In Japan, where faithful service of a master was regarded as a calling worthy of absorbing any one's highest abilities through a lifetime, the position of a servant was not menial or degrading, but might be higher than that of the farmer, merchant, or artisan. Whether the position was a high or a low one depended, not so much on the work done, as the person for whom it was done, and the servant of a daimiō or high rank samurai was worthy of more honor, and might be of far better birth, than the independent merchant or artisan. As the former feudal system is yet within the memory of many of the present generation, and its feelings still alive in Japan, much of the old sentiment remains, even with the merely hired domestics in a household of the present day. The servant, by his own master, is addressed by name, with no title of respect, is treated as an inferior, and spoken to in the language used toward inferiors; but to all others he is a person to be treated with respect, — to be bowed to profoundly, addressed by the title San, and spoken to in the politest of language. You make a call upon a Japanese household, and the servant who admits you will expect to exchange the formal salutations with you. When you are ushered into the reception-room, should the lady of the house be absent, the head servants will not only serve you with tea and refreshments and offer you hospitalities in their mistress's name, but may, if no one else be there, sit with you in the parlor, entertaining you with conversation until the return of the hostess. The servants of the household are by no means ignored socially, as they are with us, but are always recognized and saluted by visitors as they pass into and out of the room, and are free to join in the conversation of their betters, should they see any place where it is possible that they may shed light on the subject discussed. But though given this liberty of speech, treated with much consideration, and having sometimes much responsibility, servants do not forget their places in the household, and do not seem to be bold or out of place. Indeed, the manners of some of them would seem, to any one but a Japanese, to denote a lack of proper self-respect, — an excess of humility, or an affectation of it.

In explaining to my scholars, who were reading "Little Lord Fauntleroy" in English, a passage where a footman is spoken of as having nearly disgraced himself by laughing at some quaint saying of the young lord, my little peeresses were amazed beyond measure to learn that in Europe and America a servant is expected never to show any interest in, or knowledge of, the conversation of his betters, never to speak unless addressed, and never to smile under any circumstances. Doubtless, in their shrewd little brains, they formed their opinion of a civilization imposing such barbarous restraints upon one class of persons.

The women servants in a family are in position more like the self-respecting, old-fashioned New England "help" than they are like the modern "girl." They do not work all day while the mistress sits in the parlor doing nothing, and then, when their day's work is done, go out, anxious to forget, in the society of their friends, the drudgery which only the necessity for self-support and the high wages to be earned render tolerable. As has been explained in a previous chapter, the mistress of the house — be she princess or peasant — is herself the head servant, and only gives up to her helpers the part of the labor which she has not the time or strength to perform. Certain menial duties toward her husband and children, every Japanese wife and mother must do herself, and would scorn to delegate to any other woman except in case of absolute necessity. Thus there is not that gap between mistress and maid that exists in our days among the women of this country. The servants work with their mistress, helping her in every possible way, and are treated as responsible members of the household, if not of the family itself.

At evening, when the wooden shutters are slid into their places around the porch and the lamps are lighted, the family gather together in the sitting-room around the *hibachi* to talk, free from interruption, for no visitor comes at such an hour to disturb the family circle. The mother will have her sewing or work, the children will study their lessons, and the others will talk or amuse themselves in various ways. Then, perhaps, the maidservants, having finished their tasks about the house, will join the circle, — always at a respectful distance, — will do their sewing and listen to the talk, and often join in the conversation, but in the most humble manner. Perhaps, at times, some one more ambitious than the others will bring in a book, and ask the meaning of a word or a phrase she has met in studying, and little helps of this kind are given most willingly.

We have seen that the ladies-in-waiting in the houses of the nobles are daughters of samurai, who gladly serve in these positions for the sake of the honor of such service, and the training they receive in noble houses. In a somewhat similar way, places in the homes of those of distinction or skill in any art or profession are held in great demand among the Japanese; and a prominent poet, scholar, physician, or professional man of any kind is often asked by anxious parents to take their sons under his own roof, so that they may be under his influence, and receive the benefits of stay in such an honorable house. The parents who thus send their children may not be of low rank at all, but are usually not sufficiently well-to-do to spend much money in the education of their children. The position that such boys occupy in the household is a curious one. They are called *Sho-séi*, meaning students, and students they usually are, spending all their leisure moments and their evenings in study. They are never treated as inferiors, except in age and experience; they may or may not eat with the family, and are always addressed with respect. On the other hand, they always feel themselves to be dependents, and must be willing without wages to work in any capacity about the house, for the sake of picking up what crumbs of knowledge may fall to them from their master's table. Service is not absolutely demanded of them, but they are expected to do what will pay for their board, and do not regard menial work as below them, performing cheerfully all that the master may require of them.

In this way, a man of moderate means can help along many poor young men in whom he may feel interested, and in return be saved expense about his household work; and the students, while always considerately treated, are able without great expense to study, — often even to prepare for college, or get a start in one of the professions, for they have many leisure moments to devote to their books. Many prominent men of the present day have been students of this class, and are now in their turn helping the younger generation.

The boys that one sees in shops, or, with workmen of all kinds, helping in many little ways, are not hirelings, but apprentices, who hope some day to hold just as good positions as their masters, and expect to know as much, if not a great deal more. At the shop or in the home, they not only help in the trades or occupations they are learning, but are willing to do any kind of menial work for their master or his family in return for what they receive from him; for they do not pay for their board nor for what they are taught. Even when the age of education is already past, grown men and women are willing to leave quite independent positions to shine with reflected glory as servants of persons of high rank or distinction. "The servant is not greater than his master" in Japan; but if the master is great, the servant is considerably greater than the man without a master.

In a country like Japan, where one finds but few wealthy people, there may be cause for wonder at the large households, where there are so many servants. There will be often as many as ten or more servants in a home where, in other ways, luxury and wealth are not displayed. In the *oku*, or the part of the house where the lady of the house stays, are found her own maid, and women who help in the work about the house, sew in their leisure moments, and are the higher servants of the family; there are also the children's attendants, often one for each child, as well as the waiting women for the Go Inkyo Sama. In the kitchen are the cooks and their assistants, the lower servants, and usually one or more *jinrikisha* men, who belong to the house, and, if this be the home of an official who keeps horses, a *bettō* for each animal. There are also gardeners, errand-boys, and gate-keepers to guard the large *yashikis*. Such a retinue would seem a great deal to maintain; but servants' wages are so low, and the cost of living is so small, that in this matter Japanese can afford to be luxurious. Three or four dollars will cover the cost of food for a month for one person, and women servants expect only a few dollars in wages for that time. The men receive much higher pay, but at the most it is less than what a good cook receives in many homes here. The wages do not include occasional presents, especially those given semi-annually, — a small sum of money, or dress material of some kind, — which servants expect, and which, of course, are no small item in the family expense.

Homes which maintain a great deal of style need many servants, for they expect to work less than the American servant, and are less able to hurry and rush through their work; and they do not desire, if they could, to take life so hard, even to earn greater pay. The family, too, in many cases are used to having plenty of hands to do the work; the ladies are much less independent, and life has more formalities and red tape in Japan than in America. A great deal of the shopping is done by servants, who are sent out on errands and often do important business. Maids accompany their mistresses to make visits; servants go with parties to the theatre, to picnics, or on journeys, and these expeditions are as heartily enjoyed by them as by their masters. It is expected, especially of ladies and persons of high rank, that the details of the journey, the bargaining with coolies, the hiring of vehicles, and paying of bills, be left in charge of some manservant, who is entirely responsible, and who makes all the bargains, arranges the journey for his employer, and takes charge of everything, — even to the amount of fees given along the way.

Perhaps the highest positions of service now — positions honorable anywhere in Japan — are held by those who remain of the old retainers of daimiōs, and who regulate the households of the nobles. Such men must have good education, and good judgment; for much is left in their hands, and they are usually gentlemen, who would be known as such anywhere. They are the stewards of the household, the secretaries of their masters; keep all accounts, for which they are responsible, and attend to the minor affairs of etiquette, — the latter no trifling duty in a noble's home. It is they who accompany the nobles on their journeys, — regulate, advise, and attend to the little affairs of life, of which the master may be ignorant and cares not to learn. They are the last of the crowds of feudal retainers, who once filled castle and *yashiki*, and are now scattered throughout the length and breadth of the kingdom.

The higher servants in the household must be always more or less trained in etiquette, and are expected to look neat and tidy; to serve guests with tea and refreshments, without any orders to that effect; and to use their judgment in little household affairs, and thus help the lady of the house. They are usually clever with their fingers, and can sew neatly. When their mistress goes out they assist her to dress, and only a few words from her will be necessary for them to have everything in readiness, from her sash and dress to all the little belongings of a lady's costume. Many a bright, quick servant is found who will understand and guess her mistress's wants without being told each detail, and these not only serve with their hands, but think for their employers.

Much less is expected of the lower servants, who belong to the kitchen, and have less to do with the family in general, and little or no personal contact with their masters. They perform their round of duties with little responsibility, and are regarded as much lower in the social scale of servants, of which we have seen there are many degrees.

The little *gozen-taki*, or rice-cook, who works all day in the kitchen, may be a fat, red-cheeked, frowsy-haired country girl, — patient, hard-working, and humble-minded, — willing to pother about all day with her kettles and pans, and sit up half the night over her own sewing, or the study of the often unfamiliar art of reading and writing; but entirely unacquainted with the details of etiquette, a knowledge of which is a necessity to the higher servants, —

sometimes even thrown into an agony of diffidence should it become necessary to appear before master or mistress.

Some of the customs of the household, in regard to servants, are quite striking to a foreigner. When the master of the house starts out each morning, besides the wife and children who see him off, all the servants who are not especially occupied — a goodly number, sometimes — come to the front door and bow down to bid him good-by. On his return, also, when the noise of the *kuruma* is heard, and the shout of the men, who call out " *O kaéri!* " when near the house, the servants go out to greet him, and bowing low speak the customary words of salutation. To a greater or less degree, the same is done to every member of the family, the younger members, however, receiving a smaller share of the attention than their elders.

When, as very often happens, a guest staying for any length of time in a family, or a frequent visitor, gives a servant a present of money or any trifle, the servant, after thanking the donor, takes the white paper bundle to the mistress of the house, and shows it to her, expressing his gratitude to her for the gift, and also asking her to thank the giver. This, of course, is always done, for a gift to a servant is as much of a favor to the mistress as a present to a child is to its mother.

When a servant wishes to leave a family, she rarely goes to her mistress and states that she is dissatisfied with her position, and that some better chance has been offered her. Such a natural excuse never occurs to the Japanese servant, unless he be a *jinrikisha* man or *bettō*, who may not know how to do better; for it is a very rude way of leaving service. The high-minded maid will proceed very differently. A few days' leave of absence to visit home will be asked and usually granted, for Japanese servants never have any settled time to take holiday. At the end of the given time the mistress will begin to wonder what has become of the girl, who has failed to return; and the lady will make up her mind she will not let her go again so readily. Just when she has a sharp reproof ready, a messenger or letter will arrive, with some good excuse, couched in most polite and humble terms. Sometimes it will be that she has found herself too weak for service, or that work at home, or the illness of some member of the family, detains her, so that she is not able to come back at present. The excuse is understood and accepted as final, and another servant is sought for and obtained. After several weeks have passed, very likely after entering a new place, the old servant will turn up some day, express her thanks for all past kindnesses and regrets at not returning in time, will take her pay and her bundles, and disappear forever.

Even when servants come on trial for a few days, they often go away nominally to fetch their belongings, or make arrangements to return, but the lady of the house does not know whether the woman is satisfied or not. If she is not, her refusal is always brought by a third person. If the mistress, on her side, does not wish to hire the girl, she will not tell her so to her face, but will send word at this time to prevent her coming. Such is the etiquette in these matters of mistress and maid.

Only by a multiplicity of details is it possible to give much idea of the position of servants in a Japanese house, and even then the result arrived at is that the positions of what we would call domestic servants vary so greatly in honor and responsibility that it is almost impossible to draw any general conclusions upon this subject. We have seen that there is no distinct servile class in Japan, and that a person's social status is not altered by the fact that he serves in a menial capacity, provided that service be of one above him in rank and not below him. This is largely the result of the grading of society upon other lines than those on which our social distinctions are founded, and partly the result of the fact that women, of whatever class, are servants so far as persons of the opposite sex in their own class are concerned. The women of Japan to-day form the great servile class, and, as they are also the wives and mothers of those whom they serve, they are treated, of course, with a certain consideration and respect never given to a mere servant; and through them, all domestic service is elevated.

There are two employments which I have mentioned among those of domestic servants because they would be so classed by us, but which in Japan rank among the trades. The *jinrikisha* man and the groom belong, as a rule, to a certain class at the bottom of the social ladder, and no samurai would think of entering either of these occupations, except under stress of severest poverty. The *bettōs*, or grooms, are a hereditary class and a regular guild, and have a reputation, among both Japanese and foreigners, as a betting, gambling, cheating, good-for-nothing lot. An honest *bettō* is a rare phenomenon. The *jinrikisha* men are, many of them, sons of peasants, who come to the cities for the sake of earning more money, or leading a livelier life than can be found in the little thatched cottage among the rice-fields. Few of them are married, or have homes of their own. Many of them drink and gamble, and sow their wild oats in all possible ways; but they are a well-meaning, fairly honest, happy-go-lucky set, who lead hard lives of exhausting labor, and endure long hours of exposure to heat and cold, rain, snow, and blinding sunshine, not only with little complaint or grumbling, but with absolute cheerfulness and hilarity. A strong, fast *jinrikisha* man takes great pride in his strength and speed. It is a point of honor with him to pull his passenger up the steepest and most slippery of hills, and never to heed him if he expresses a desire to walk in order to save his man. I have had my *kurumaya* stoutly refuse, again and again, my offers to walk up a steep hill, even when the snow was so soft and slippery under his bare feet that he fell three times in making the ascent. "*Dai jobu*" (safe) would be his smiling response to all my protestations; and, once in a *jinrikisha*, the passenger is entirely at the mercy of his man in all matters of getting into and out of the vehicle. But though the *jinrikisha* man is, for the time being, the autocrat and controlling power over his passenger, and though he will not obey the behests of his employer, except so far as they seem reasonable and in accordance with the best interests of all concerned, he constitutes himself the protector and assistant, the adviser and counselor, of him whom he serves, and gives his best thought and intelligence, as well as his speed and strength, to the service in which he is engaged. If he thinks it safe, he will tear like an unbroken colt through the business portions of the city, knocking bundles out of the hands of foot passengers, or even hitting the wayfarers themselves in a fierce dash through their midst, laughing gayly at their protests, and at threats of wrath to come from his helpless passenger; but should hint of insult or injury against *kuruma*, passenger, or passenger's dog fall upon his ears, he will drop the *jinrikisha* shafts, and administer condign punishment to the offender, unchecked by thoughts of the ever-present police, or by any terrors that his employer may hold over his head. In no other country in the world, perhaps, can a lady place more entire confidence in the honor and loyalty of her servant than she can in Japan in her *kurumaya*, whether he be her private servant, or one from a respectable stand. He may not do what she bids him, but that is quite a secondary matter. He will study her interests; will remember her likes and dislikes; will take a mental inventory of the various accessories or bundles that she carries with her, and will never permit her to lose or forget one of them; will run his legs off in her service, and defend her and her property valiantly in case of need. Of course, as in all classes there are different grades, so there are *jinrikisha* men who seem to have sunk so low in their calling that they have lost all feeling of loyalty to their employer, and only care selfishly for the pittance they gain. Such men are often found in the treaty ports, eagerly seeking for the rich foreigner, from whom they can get an extra fee, and whom they regard as outside of their code of morals, and hence as their natural prey. Travelers, and even residents of Japan, have often complained of such treatment; and it is only after long stay in Japan, among the Japanese themselves, that one can tell what a *jinrikisha* man is capable of.

If you employ one *kurumaya* for any length of time, you come to have a real affection for him on account of his loyal, faithful, cheerful service, such as we seldom find in this country except when inspired by personal feeling. When you have ridden miles and miles, by night and by day, through rain and sleet and hottest sunshine, behind a man who has used every power of body and mind in your service, you cannot but have a strong feeling of affection toward him, and of pride in him as well. It is something the feeling that one has for a good saddle-horse, but more developed. You rejoice, not only in his strength and speed, put forth so willingly in your service; in his picturesque, dark blue costume with your monogram embroidered on the back; in his handsomely turned ankles; in his black, wavy hair; in his delicate hands and trim waist, — though these are often a source of pride to you, — but his skill in divining your wants; his use of his tongue in your service; his helping out of your faltering Japanese with explanations which, if not elegant, have the merit of being easily understood; his combats with extortionate shopkeepers in your behalf; his interest in all your doings and concerns, — remain as a pleasant memory, upon your return to a land where no man would so far forget his manhood as to give himself so completely and without reserve to the service of any master save Mammon.

As old Japan, with its quaintness, its mediæval flavor, its feudalism, its loyalty, its sense of honor, and its transcendental contempt for money and luxury, recedes into the past, and as the memories of my life there grow dim, two figures stand out more and more boldly from the fading background, — both, the figures of faithful servants. One, Yasaku, the *kurumaya*, a very Hercules, who could keep close to a pair of coach horses through miles of city streets, and who never suffered mortal *jinrikisha* man to pass him. My champion in all times of danger and alarm, but a very autocrat in all minor matters, — his cheery face, his broad shoulders with their blue draperies, his jolly, boyish voice, and his dainty, delicate hands come before me as I write, and I wonder to what fortunate person he is now giving the intelligent service that he once gave so whole-heartedly to me. The other, O Kaio, my maid, her plain little face, with its upturned eyes, growing, as the days went by, absolutely beautiful in the light of pure goodness that beamed from it. A Japanese Christian, with all the Christian virtues well developed, she became to me not only a good servant, doing her work with conscientious fidelity, but a sympathetic friend, to whom I turned for help in time of need; and whom I left, when I returned to America, with a sincere sorrow in my heart at parting with one who had grown to fill so large a place in my thoughts. Her little, half-shy, half-motherly ways toward her big foreign mistress had a charm all their own. Her pride and delight over my progress in the language; her patient efforts to make me understand new words, or to understand my uncouth foreign idioms; her joy, when at last I reached the point where a story told by her lips could be comprehended and enjoyed, — gave a continual encouragement in a task too often completely disheartening.

During the last summer of my stay in Japan, cutting loose from all foreigners and foreign associations, I traveled alone with her through the heart of the country, stopping only at Japanese hotels, and carrying with me no supplies to eke out the simple Japanese fare. Through floods and typhoons we journeyed. Long days of scorching heat or driving rain in no way abated her cheerfulness, or lessened her desire to do all that she could for my aid and comfort. Not one sad look nor impatient word showed a flaw in her perfect temper; and if she privately made up her mind that I was crazy, she never by word or look gave a hint of her thought. *Jinrikisha* men grumbled and gave out; hotel-keepers resented the presence of my dog, or presented extortionate bills; but O Kaio's good temper and tact never failed her. Difficulties were smoothed away; bills were compromised and reduced; the dog slept securely by my side on a red blanket in the best rooms of the best hotels; and O Kaio smiled, told her quaint stories, amused me and ministered to me, as if I were her one object in life, though husband and children were far away in distant Tōkyō, and her mother's heart yearned for her little ones.

EPILOGUE.

My task is ended. One half of Japan, with its virtues and its frailties, its privileges and its wrongs, has been brought, so far as my pen can bring it, within the knowledge of the American public. If, through this work, one person setting forth for the Land of the Rising Sun goes better prepared to comprehend the thoughts, the needs, and the virtues of the noble, gentle, self-sacrificing women who make up one half the population of the Island Empire, my labor will not have been in vain.

INDEX.

Adoption, 103, 112, 113, 187.
Agility of Japanese, 13.
Amado, sliding wooden shutters, used to inclose a Japanese house at night, 23.
Andon, a standing lamp inclosed in a paper case, 89.
Ané San, elder sister (San, the honorific), a title used by the the younger children in a family in speaking to their eldest sister, 20.
Aoyama, 131.
Apprentices, 309, 310.
Art in common things, 237-239.
Artisans, 235-239, 270.

Babyhood, 1-17; bathing, 10; conditions of life, 6, 7; dress, 6, 15; food, 10, 11; imperial babies, 8, 9; learning to talk, 16; learning to walk, 13, 14; of lower classes, 7; of middle classes, 8; of nobility, 8; skin troubles, 11; teething, 12; tied to the back, 7, 8, 12.
Baths, public, 10.
Beauty, Japanese standard of, 58; early loss of, 122.
Bé-bé, a child's word for dress, 16.
Betrothal, 60.
Bettō, a groom or footman who cares for the horse in the stable and runs ahead of it in the road, 62, 71, 311, 316, 319.
Birth, 1.
Breakfast, 89.
Buddhism, 168, 240; introduction of, 143-145.
Buddhist funeral, 131, 132.
Buddhist nuns, 155.

Castles, 151, 157, 169, 171, 173, 174, 185, 186, 192.
Chadai, literally "tea money," the fee given at an inn, 251-253.
Cherry blossoms, 28, 146, 166, 176, 177, 191, 295, 296.
Childhood. See Girlhood.
Children, Japanese compared with American, 19; intellectual characteristics of Japanese, 41.
Chinese characters, 40.
Chinese civilization introduced, 142.
Chinese code of morals, 103, 111.
Christianity, 77, 81, 168, 206, 207.
Chrysanthemum, 166, 296-298.
Civilization, new, 77.
Concubinage, 85, 111.
Confectionery, 146.
Confucius, 103, 168.
Constitution, promulgation of the, 114, 276.
Corea, conquest of, 139-143.
Country and city, 278, 279.
Court, after conquest of Corea, 143-146; amusements, 145; costumes, 146; in early times, 138, 139; ladies, 145, 148, 152-154; life, 138-168; of daimiō, 171; of Shōgun, 170, 171; removal to Tōkyō, 156.
Courtship, 58.
Crucifixion, 199, 234.

Dai jobu, "Safe," "All right," 320.
Daimiō, a member of the landed nobility under the feudal system, 169-195; his castles, 169, 173; his courts, 171; his daughters, 175, 177, 180, 182-184, 191, 192-195; his journeys to Yedo, 171-173; his retainers, 169, 171, 173, 175, 177-179, 181, 183, 185, 186; his wife, 175, 177, 182, 192-195; seclusion of, 172-174.

INDEX.

Dancing, 38, 287, 288.
Dancing girls. See Géisha.
Dango Zaka, 296.
Dashi, a float used in festival processions, 275-278.
Decency, Japanese standard of, 255-260.
Deformity, caused by position in sitting, 9.
Divorce, among lower classes, 66, 69, 73; among higher classes, 66, 68; right of, granted to women, 66; right to children in case of, 67, 105.
Dolls, feast of, 28-31.
Dress, baby, 6, 15; court, 145, 146; girl's, 15; in daimiōs' houses, 187, 192; military, of samurai women, 188; of lower classes, 126, 127, 128; of pilgrims, 243; showing age of wearer, 119.

Education of girls, 37-56; difficulties in new system, 52-56; fault in Japanese system, 39; in old times, 37.
Education, higher, a doubtful help, 79; effect on home life, 77; producing repugnance to marriage, 80.
Education of daimiō's daughter, 177-180.
Embroidered robes, 95, 146, 188, 192.
Emperor, 111, 114, 134, 151-153, 155-157, 161, 164-166, 292.
Emperors, after introduction of Chinese civilization, 143-145; children of, 164; daughters of, 155; early retirement of, 134; in early times, 138; seclusion of, 143-145, 155, 156, 161, 169.
Empress, 88, 115, 140, 150-168.
Empress dowager, 152.
Engawa, the piazza that runs about a Japanese house, 23.
Etiquette, court, 153; in daimiōs' houses, 177-179; in the home, 19, 20; instruction in, 46, 47; of leaving service, 316, 317; towards servants, 304, 305.

Fairy tales, 32.
Family, organization of, 139.

Fancy work, 95.
Father's relation to children, 100.
Festivals: of dolls, 28; of flowers, 27, 99, 295-297; of the new year, 25; temple, 270-278.
Feudal system, 169.
Feudal times, pictures of, 190-192; stories of, 184-187.
Flirtation, unknown to Japanese girls, 34.
Flower arrangement, 42.
Flower painting, 47.
Flower shows, 270-272.
Fortune-telling, 281-285.
Fuji, 58, 242.
Funeral service, 131, 132.

Games: battledore and shuttlecock, 31; at court, 145; Go, 136; hyaku nin ishu, 26; shogi, 136.
Géisha, a professional dancing and singing girl, 286-289.
Géisha ya, an establishment where géishas may be hired, 286.
Géta, a wooden clog, 13, 14.
Ginza, 265.

Haori, a coat of cotton, silk, or crape, worn over the kimono, 8.
Hara-kiri, suicide by stabbing in the abdomen, 201, 202.
Haru Ko, 155-168.
Haru, Prince, 113, 152.
Héimin, the class of farmers, artisans, and merchants, 203, 228, 229.
Héimin, class characteristics of, 229-240.
Hibachi, a brazier for burning charcoal, 30, 72, 136, 307.
Hidéyoshi. See Toyotomi.
Hinin, a class of paupers, 228.
Hiyéi Zan, 243.
Holidays, 269.
Hotels, 247-250.
Hotel-keepers, 280, 281.
Household duties, training for, 21.
Hyaku nin ishu, "Poems of a hundred poets," the name of a game, 26.

Instruction in etiquette, 46; in flower arranging, 42; in flower painting, 47; in music, 41; in reading and writing, 38; in tea ceremony, 44.
Inkyo, a place of retirement, the home of a person who has retired from active life, 136.
Inu, a dog, 250.
Isé, 231.
Iwafuji, 210-213.
Iwakura, Prince, 157.
Iya, a child's word, denoting dislike or negation, 16.
Iyémitsŭ, 171, 172.
Iyéyasŭ, 169.

"Japan Mail," 159.
Japanese language, 16, 40, 179.
Japanese literature, 147-150.
Jimmu Tenno, 138.
Jingu Kōgō, 139-143, 147.
Jinrikisha, a light carriage drawn by one or more men, and which will hold one or two persons, 26, 70, 92, 268, 272, 320, 321.
Jinrikisha man, 26, 62, 69, 92, 108, 270, 279, 299, 316, 319-324.
Jōrō, a prostitute, 289-292.
Jōrōya, a house of prostitution, 290-292.

Kaméido, 296.
Kakémono, a hanging scroll, 44, 147, 238.
Katsuobushi, a kind of dried fish, 5.
Kimono, a long gown with wide sleeves, and open in front, worn by Japanese of all classes, 7, 94, 188, 192, 287.
Kisses, 36.
Knees, flexibility of, 9.
Kotatsu, a charcoal fire in a brazier or a small fireplace in the floor, over which a wooden frame is set, and the whole covered by a quilt, 33.
Koto, a musical instrument, 42.
Kugé, the court nobility, 155, 170.
Kura, a fireproof storehouse, 147, 171, 173.
Kuruma, a wheeled vehicle of any kind, used as synonymous with jinrikisha, which see.
Kurumaya, one who pulls a kuruma. See Jinrikisha man.
Kurushima, 203.
Kyōtō, 156, 171, 240, 241.

Ladies, court, 145, 148, 152-154; of daimiōs' families, 175-180, 182-184.
Ladies-in-waiting, 180-182, 224.
Loyalty, 33, 75, 197, 206-208, 217, 302-304.

Mam ma, a baby's word for rice or food, 16.
Manners of children, 18.
Marriage, 57-83; ceremony, 61, 63; feast, 63; festivities after, 63, 64; guests, 63; presents, 62; registration, 65; to yoshii, 104; trousseau, 61.
Marumagi, a style of arranging the hair of married ladies, 119.
Matsuri, a festival, usually in honor of some god, 274-278.
Méiji (Enlightened Rule), the name of the era that began with the accession of the present Emperor in 1868, 149.
Mékaké, a concubine, 111-114.
Men, old, dependence of, 133; amusements of, 136.
Merchants, 262-269.
Military service of women, 188-190, 208, 223.
Missionary schools, 56.
Miya maéri, the presentation of a child at the temple on the thirtieth day after birth, 3-6.
Mochi, a kind of rice cake, 5, 24, 25, 65.
Momotaro, 33.
Morality, standards of, 76.
Mother, her relation to children, 99-102.
Mother-in-law, 84, 87; O Kiku's, 74.
Mukōjima, 191, 295.
Musical instruments, 41, 42.

Names, 3.
Nara, 247.
Nikkō, 231, 245.
No, a pantomimic dance, 292, 293.
Norimono, a palanquin, 30.

INDEX.

Noshi, a bit of dried fish, usually folded in colored paper, given with a present for good luck, 2.
Nursing the sick, 101.

O, an honorific used before many nouns, and before most names of women, 20.
O Bā San, grandmother, 124.
O Bă San, aunt, 124.
Obi, a girdle or sash, 60.
Occupations of the blind, 42; of the court, 143-150, 165, 166; of the daimios' ladies, 175-180; of the Empress, 156-166; of old people, 136, 120-122, 124-128; of old samurai women, 223, 224; of servants, 299, 304, 306, 308-315, 318; of women, 108-110, 85-103, 242-256, 279-292, 306, 318; of young girls, 21-34, 38-47.
O Haru, 211-213.
Oishi, 198, 214.
Oji, 296.
O Jo Sama, young lady, 20.
O kaeri, "Honorable return," a greeting shouted by the attendant, upon the master's or mistress's return to the house, 100, 315.
O Kaio, 324-326.
O Kiku's marriage and divorce, 73, 74.
Old age, privileges of, 120, 122, 123; provision for, 134.
Old men, 133, 136.
O miage, a present given on returning from a journey or pleasure excursion, 274.
Oni, a devil or goblin, 33.
Onoyé, 210-213.

Palace, new, 151-153.
Parents, duties to, 134; respect for, 133.
Parents-in-law, 84, 87.
Peasant women, 108, 240-261.
Peasantry, 228-240.
Physicians' fees, 204.
Pilgrims, 241, 242.
Pillow, 89.
Pleasure excursions, 99.
Poems of a hundred poets, 26.
Poetry, 26, 148-150.

Presents, 96; after a wedding, 65; at betrothal, 60; at miya maéri, 4; at weddings, 62; how wrapped, 2; in honor of a birth, 1; of eggs, 2, 5; of money, 204, 205; on returning from a journey, 274; on the thirtieth day after birth, 5; to servants, 311, 315.
Prostitutes. See Jōrō.
Prostitution, houses of, 114, 214, 290.
Purity of Japanese women, 216-219.

Retirement from business, 133.
Retirement of emperors, 134.
Revenge, 198, 210-214.
Revolution of 1868, 76, 221.
Rice, red bean, 3, 5, 65.
Rin, one tenth of a sen, or about one mill, 240.
Rōnin, a samurai who has lost his master and owes no allegiance to any daimiō, 198, 213.

Sakaki, the Cleyera Japonica, 98.
Saké, wine made from rice, 22, 63, 136, 296; white, 29.
Sama, or San, an honorific placed after names, equivalent to Mr., Mrs., or Miss, 20, 73, 124, 136, 232, 283, 284, 304.
Samisen, a musical instrument, 42, 127, 277, 286.
Samurai, the military class, 42, 75, 76, 105, 169, 174, 175, 180, 196-227, 232, 263, 302, 303, 307, 319; character of, 197-207; spirit of, 199, 205.
Samurai girls in school, 226.
Samurai women, character of, 207-223; present work of, 223-327.
Satsuma rebellion, the, 222.
School system, the, 50.
School, the Peeress's, 150, 162, 163, 182.
Schools, missionary, 56.
Self-possession of Japanese girls, 47.
Self-sacrifice, 214-219.
Sen, one hundredth part of a yen, value about one cent, 240, 273, 298.

Servants, characteristics of, 299-302; duties of, 302-315; in employ of foreigners, 299-302; number employed, 310, 311; position of, 302-310; wages of, 311.
Sewing, 23, 94.
Shinto, 4, 155.
Shogi, Japanese chess, 136.
Shōgun, the Tycoon, the Viceroy, or so-called temporal ruler of Japan under the feudal system, 155, 169, 171, 173, 176, 185, 186, 191, 194, 197, 208, 224, 231-234, 292; daughter of, 176, 194.
Shōgunate, 155, 190, 192, 221, 222.
Shoji, sliding windows covered with paper, 23, 71.
Shopping, 264-268.
Sho-séi, a student, 308.
Silk-mosaic, 95, 192.
Silkworms, 95, 246.
Soroban, an abacus, 266-268.
Sumida River, 173, 295.

Tabi, a mitten-like sock, 13.
Ta ta, a baby's word for sock or tabi, 16.
Taiko Sama. See Toyotomi.
Tea, 91, 92; ceremonial, 44, 136, 176.
Tea-gardens, 247.
Tea-houses, 250-255.
Teachers' pay, 204.
Teaching. See Instruction.
Teeth, blackened after marriage, 63.
Temple, 4, 120, 129, 240.
Theatre, 33, 99, 292-294.
Titles used in families, 20.
Toes, prehensile, 15.
Toilet apparatus, 30.
Tōkaidō, 241.
Tokonoma, the raised alcove in a Japanese room, 44.
Tokugawa, 29, 151, 155, 231.
Tōkyō, 49, 69-71, 108, 115.
" Tōkyō Mail," 231.
Tombs, visits to, 98.

Toyotomi Hidéyoshi, 232.
Training-school for nurses, 158.
Utsunomiya, 70, 71.
Uyéno Park, 296.

Virtue, Japanese and Western ideas of, 215-219.
Visits, after marriage, 63; in honor of a birth, 1, 2; New Year's, 25; to parents, 98; to tombs of ancestors, 98.

Wakamatsu, 208, 222.
Wedding. See Marriage.
Widows, childless, 123.
Wife, childless, 102; duties of, 85-99; in great houses, 92; relation to husband, 84; relation to parents-in-law, 84; social relations, 91.
Woman's Christian Temperance Union, 114.
Women, in the city, 279-298; occupations of, 85-103, 108-110, 242-256, 306, 318; position of, 17-22, 35, 36, 57, 65-68, 76-88, 90, 91, 93, 99-118, 120-124, 132, 133, 139, 143, 145, 146, 148, 168, 189, 190, 208, 216-219, 223-227, 242-247, 260, 261, 279, 292, 298, 306, 318; purity of, 216-219.
Women, old, appearance of, 119, 122, 124, 126; examples of, 124, 126-129; in Japanese pictures, 132.

Yamato Daké, 215.
Yasaku, 324; marriage and divorce of, 69.
Yasé, 243, 244.
Yashiki, a daimiō's mansion and grounds, 169, 171, 173, 311, 313.
Yedo. See Tōkyō.
Yoshii, an adopted son, 104.
Yumoto, 245.

Zori, a straw sandal, 13.